10-18-73

The
Money
Story

Primitive money. Top to bottom: (left) string of coconut discs and shells, New Guinea; tin hat, Siam; (centre) brick of tea, China; copper ingot, Congo Free State; knife, China; dogs' teeth necklace; (right) copper dagger, Congo Free State; curved manilla bar, West Africa

The Money Story

J P Jones
FIB FREconS

Drake Publishers Inc
New York

ISBN 87749-294-8

Published in 1973 by
DRAKE PUBLISHERS INC
381 Park Avenue South,
New York, N.Y. 10016

Printed in Great Britain

1773354

CONTENTS

ILLUSTRATIONS

The painting on page 90 of The Embarkation of Henry VIII is reproduced by gracious permission of Her Majesty the Queen

The publishers wish to express their gratitude to the people and organisations acknowledged above for their help with the illustrations

To my grandchildren
Henrietta, Rebecca and Philip

1 Barter to Money of All Sorts

BARTER is trade by exchanging goods and the world's first business transaction was probably a barter deal that took place one day in the distant past when a primitive man, who hunted for a living, decided to exchange his surplus animal skins for cooking-pots, spears and arrowheads.

His progress was largely a matter of chance. He had to find tribes who made pots and spears, who had more of these articles than they required at the time and who were prepared to exchange them for his skins. Success in barter trade depends on this double coincidence of wants, as it is known, but despite the difficulties, the simple system suited the needs of primitive peoples.

The next stage in the development of barter was the selection of commodities that were always in steady demand by the people—articles which were durable and which retained their quality. The Ancient Britons found this quality in flint, invaluable to them for lighting fires and making weapons; and, in Europe, long before man learnt to till the land, itinerant traders travelled far and wide with amber from the Baltic and shells from the Atlantic coasts, which have been found thousands of miles from their places of origin.

The earliest form of barter is probably what is called the

'silent trade', in which those taking part have no direct contact. Articles to be exchanged are placed in a forest clearing and 'bargaining' is carried out by increasing or reducing the goods on offer until both parties are satisfied. While one tribe is attending to this operation the other remains hidden in the forest but keeps a watchful eye on the proceedings.

Natives in Central Africa and in the Kanaka Settlements of New Guinea still conduct their business by the 'silent trade' and it is interesting to note that by using this method members of the recent Hovercraft expedition up the Amazon made contact with primitive people who had never before set eyes on a white man.

Those who adhere to the 'silent trade' are not without money to make their purchases. Money circulates in these areas but the natives *prefer* to barter. They find the often lengthy bargaining stimulating and amusing and, from centuries of experience, they know the precise exchange value of their goods and they are not as affected by price fluctuations as people who live in more advanced parts of the world.

As civilisation progressed men moved about more freely and more goods became available but the difficulties of coinciding individual wants were intensified. With trade confined to barter, improvement in living standards was slow and uncertain. Each family and tribe produced mainly to meet its own requirements and their lives were occasionally enriched by the exchange of products with others. The need was for some generally accepted means of payment in which goods could be sold at an agreed price and the payment spent on other goods of their own choosing. Like the domestication of animals and the cultivation of the land, the development of money is part of the evolution of human society. It was a vital prerequisite in the transition from subsistence living to specialised production of goods and the division of labour.

As time went on barter transactions became more involved and men acquired the habit of calculating the value of an article in terms of some standard commodity always in steady demand. We believe that ancient peoples chose the ox as the first measure of value. We know that cattle served this purpose at the time of Homer. The word 'pecuniary', meaning 'of or in money', comes from *pecunia*, the Latin for 'money', which in turn stems from *pecus*, meaning cattle. Primitive people in Siberia and parts of Africa and South America have used cattle as money for countless generations. Even today in the remote areas of the Caucasus people regard their cattle as money and price other things in terms of cows or a fraction of a cow.

Other things besides cattle were used as a means of exchange and a measure of value. Thousands of years ago the Chinese settled their transactions with a variety of tools and bolts of cloth, and 3,000 years before the birth of Christ the Babylonians used such diverse things as gold and silver, honey, wool, leather and paper to make their payments.

Since earliest times grain was a popular form of money used in many parts of the world. For several centuries after Christ, Egyptian kings accepted grain in payment of rent and taxes. The grain was stored in large granaries and in a sense these stores were the world's first banks. The farmer could deposit his grain in the store whenever he liked and draw a kind of cheque on the store, which would be honoured if the farmer had enough grain in his 'account'. Although coins circulated in Egypt at the time, the grain banks continued to flourish because they offered a convenient service to the thousands of small farmers in the Nile Delta.

Until the nineteenth century many farmers in Britain paid their rent in grain. The landlord took as his rent the grain left over after the farmer had consumed what he needed and what he kept as seed for the next harvest. The quantity of grain handed to the landlord, which varied with the size and fertility of the farm, was the basis on which rent was calculated in this country up to the Industrial Revolution. To this day rents vary with the fertility and acreage of the farm with some adjustment for the standard of the farmhouse and buildings.

Although modern money circulates in their countries many Chinese, Indians, Mexicans and natives of the Philippines still use grain to make their purchases. In parts of the Philippines

13

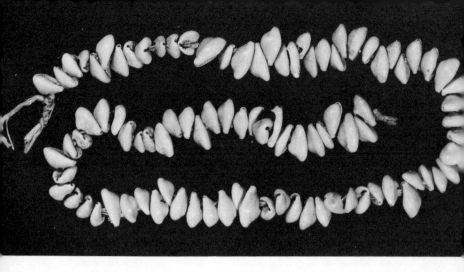

String of cowrie shells used as primitive money in the Pacific Ocean islands

wages are paid in rice at the rate of so many handsful a day and shopkeepers quote their prices in handsful of rice.

The Romans used salt to pay their workmen's wages and the word 'salary' comes from the Latin *salarium*, meaning salt. Roadmen in the Congo are still paid with salt, indispensable to them to flavour their food, which is often almost tasteless. Travellers in the mountainous hinterland of New Guinea say that the natives there are so salt hungry that they will kill for it without hesitation. They will sell anything for salt and most of them will accept no other currency.

Miniature models of tools and implements were the earliest form of currency in certain parts of the world. In Japan they used arrowheads made from jewels for ceremonial purposes and the New Guinea natives used mother-of-pearl fish-hooks too frail to catch fish. Excavations in northern Europe have brought to light stone axes too small and delicate for any purpose other than as ornaments or as money.

The best-known ornamental money was the cowrie shell found mainly on the beaches of the Pacific Ocean islands. People living in this remote part of the world had no food or clothing problems. They were mainly preoccupied with finding ways of decorating themselves. On the seashores they collected the pretty, glistening straw-coloured cowrie shells and strung them together like beads. So attractive were the shells that those who gathered them found other people who were willing to give them food in exchange. As the shells become more popular people began to work harder to increase their crops so that they could exchange their surplus grain and vegetables for the shells.

Before long and entirely by accident the natives discovered that they were using money—something willingly accepted in exchange for goods. It was also a store of wealth and a man's riches could be measured by the number of cowrie necklaces he wore. The shells were strung on cane strips of varying lengths, and the prices of other commodities were quoted in these lengths.

We believe that people used cowries as currency in India, China and the Middle East for thousands of years before Christ and in later times they circulated in the greater parts of the continents of Africa and Asia and all through the Pacific Islands. Only a generation ago natives used cowries as money on the west coast of Africa, where 5,000 shells were worth one Indian rupee—then about a shilling. The cowrie is still not completely extinct. So important was it as a currency that, when the Japanese invaded New Guinea in 1942 and handed out cowrie shells so recklessly that their value fell sharply, it threatened to disrupt the financial stability of the island.

Like the Chinese, people in northern Europe also used tool money and this system spread to the Mediterranean and the Middle East. The Greeks used tools like spits, basins and axes to make their payments. Made originally of bronze, they were later changed to iron. Two modern Greek money units, the *obolus* and the *drachma*, derive their names from one iron spit and six iron spits.

Money can be anything that does the work of money and, to do this effectively, the unit chosen must perform three functions. It has to be a means of exchange (ie freely accepted in exchange for goods and services), a measure of value which serves as a yardstick to assess the value of other commodities, and a store of wealth. Such dissimilar units as a cow and a Pacific cowrie shell each possesses the three attributes of money and the same can be said of the many strange and unlikely things that have func-

15

tioned as money in different parts of the world over the centuries.

To perform this function the unit must possess value in itself and, to have value in an economic sense, there must be an element of scarcity. This is obvious in many cases but not so apparent in others. On the Pacific beaches there are untold millions of shells but supplies of cowrie shells for use as money were not unlimited. Before they could serve this purpose the natives had to search for them, collect them, bore holes with primitive tools and string them together as beads. The combined factors of scarcity and human endeavour created the value in the shells that enabled them to function as money.

While supplies were controlled the shells retained their value but when supplies became out of control—as occurred when the Japanese flooded New Guinea with shells during the 1939-45 war—the value dropped to a point when they became almost useless. The same thing happened when tobacco was ruled the official currency during the early colonial days in America. Attracted by the high prices growers increased their crops and the price fell so low that tobacco ceased to operate as money.

Down the centuries many bizarre things have been used for this purpose in various parts of the world but every unit—however odd—has possessed the qualities necessary to function as money.

In Fiji, the natives used porpoise teeth in this way—and still do in some localities. At one time on the island of San Cristobel they used dogs' teeth money and thousands of dogs were reared for this purpose. On the remote Pacific islands far from the march of civilisation there were many strange kinds of money—snails, the scalps of woodpeckers, birds' head feathers, eggs, pigs and sandalwood. On the island of Alor they used kettle-drums—humorously called the world's first 'sound' money—and in Borneo the currency was once human skulls.

Undoubtedly the strangest and most unwieldy form was the stone money of the Pacific Island of Yap. This consisted of discs made from quarried material called aragonite, which varied in diameter from about a foot to twelve feet. The natives drilled holes in the stones and carried them on poles. The stones would buy anything and remained in use as currency until the outbreak of the Second World War.

The stones of Yap operated efficiently as currency because they possessed the element of scarcity. The aragonite from which the money was made was a *special* kind of stone which the natives obtained from Pèlew and Guam, two islands some distance from Yap. The stones were scarce in Yap because it was difficult and dangerous to carry them in the frail native boats and many sank on their way across. The stones were also expensive to quarry because the rulers of Pelew and Guam demanded costly presents in return for permission to extract the stone.

For the purpose of 'change' smaller articles, such as strings of beads, coconuts and tobacco circulated with the large stones. Nowadays the people of Yap use American and Japanese money but this has been accepted with reluctance. Outside many of the houses you will see large stones used as ornaments, but still regarded by the natives as being of real value.

In parts of Melanesia in the Pacific Ocean the natives use what is known as 'fuse' money, so-called because their unit is a tightly wrapped packet of a hundred shillings, which looks like a stick of dynamite. The natives accept this 'fuse' money without question and will have nothing to do with paper money. When they make large purchases they pass on packets that have never been opened. This makes it easy for unscrupulous people to cheat them by making up packets containing worthless discs of the same size and weight as a shilling.

Before we leave the subject of barter it is interesting to note that as late as the middle of the nineteenth century many British factory owners opened what were known as tommy shops on or near their factory premises. The workers were compelled to buy goods on credit at the stores and the cost was set off against their wages. In this way the workers had only limited control over the wages they earned but these unsatisfactory conditions came to an end with the passing of the Truck Act in 1887, which compelled employers to pay wages in cash.

We believe that the first money freely accepted in exchange for goods and services was the Pacific cowrie shell. But the first

Greek coins 8th to 5th centuries BC: 1 electrum stater of Lydia, obverse showing forepart of lion; 2 silver stater of Corinth, obverse showing winged horse Pegasus; 3 electrum tetradrachm of Athens, obverse showing the Athenian owl

purpose-made money in the modern sense originated in China during the Chou Dynasty, which ruled from the twelfth to the third century BC. We have seen how the Chinese of that time used a variety of tools and lengths of cloth as money, and you can imagine how inconvenient it must have been to make large payments with these articles. If a man wanted to buy something expensive, like a piece of land, he would have to hire an army of coolies with handcarts to make the payment.

The Chinese solved the problem about the year 1200 BC, when the government made small metal *models* of the spades, chisels and knives and the people used these miniatures in place of the articles themselves. The idea was very popular but people still found the models too heavy to carry and, because of their varying shapes, too difficult to count. The government reduced the size of the models and made them round to make counting easier. The coins had a hole in the middle so that they could be strung together. They called the coins *cash* and we still use this word today. The Chinese continued to mint their coins with a hole.

Metal discs made in the thirteenth century BC and since discovered in Crete may have been used as coins, but the earliest European coins in the modern sense appeared in Lydia, Asia Minor, during the ninth or eighth centuries BC. We believe that merchants made these coins, but soon the governments took over manufacture of the coinage and, between the eighth and fifth centuries BC, a number of states and cities in Greece and in Asia Minor issued coins with their own emblems. Coins made in Lydia bore a lion's head, those from Corinth showed a winged horse and the Athenian coins had the emblem of an owl.

These early coins were made of electrum, a very precious alloy of gold and silver, and, for this reason, even the smallest coin was too valuable for normal payments. The electrum coins were used by merchants of the time to finance transactions between cities.

The first wholly silver coins were minted in the Greek island of Aegina around 750 BC and the first coins made entirely of gold are attributed to Croesus, the sixth-century king of Lydia. He was a very wealthy man and this is why we still say: 'As rich as Croesus'.

At that time and for several hundred years afterwards Greece was the only European country that minted coins. They were made from gold and silver; the first bronze coins did not appear until the fifth century BC.

When the Greeks used coins to replace the barter system they measured their value in terms of the goods they would buy, which is the opposite of what we do today. They minted coins with different impressions—each one used for a different purpose. One bearing an olive branch would buy a certain quantity of olive oil; another impressed with a sheep's head, so many sheep, and so on. The coins would buy no more or no less. It did not matter whether the supply of sheep was plentiful or scarce, the price always remained the same.

The Greeks later minted silver coins that were small enough to use in the retail trade and to pay wages. In this way they brought the benefits of money to more and more people. By the

19

fifth century BC many slaves were employed in Athens. They worked for their food and shelter but, when they received their wages in cash, they could buy their own food. This brought about a feeling of independence and a desire for freedom. Many former slaves became wage-earning freemen of the city and enjoyed the full rights and privileges of citizenship.

The earliest bronze coins were minted in Sicily in the fifth century BC. They appeared a little later in Athens. During the Peloponesian War the government's financial needs brought about this change in currency and many others that followed. They found that gold was more convenient than silver to settle large transactions and that bronze coins were better for small payments. Gold and bronze coins were used increasingly in the fourth century BC.

Alexander the Great introduced to all the territories he conquered a uniform coinage based on the Athenian system. He confiscated the gold and silver treasures in these countries and minted coins from them. With the sudden increase in the number of coins in circulation and no corresponding growth in the volume of goods and services, prices rose violently. This may have been the first recorded example of inflation in the world.

Alexander's contribution to the development of the coinage system is now a matter of history. Even when he was dead a tribute was paid by placing an image of his head on coins in place of the earlier city emblems. This was the first time in history that the head of a ruler appeared on a coin.

At this time the Romans were developing their own money system but it was not as advanced as in Greece. Until the third century BC the only coins in circulation were made of crude bronze. In 268 BC the Romans struck their first silver coin, called the *denarius*, and this coin became the basis of the Roman monetary system.

It is said that, in gratitude for advice given to them during the Pyrrhic War by Juno, the patron goddess of Carthage, the Romans gave her the title of *moneta* and installed their first mint in her temple on the Capitol, in Rome. It is thought that our word 'money' stems from *moneta* and is of Carthaginian origin.

Roman coins showing the twelve Caesars (1-9 silver denarii, 10-12 gold aurei): 1 Julius Caesar, 2 Augustus, 3 Tiberius, 4 Caligula, 5 Claudius, 6 Nero, 7 Galba, 8 Otho, 9 Vitellius, 10 Vespasian, 11 Titus, 12 Domitian

The Romans stamped their early coins with figures representing gods and heroes but, about a hundred years later, they were replaced by theme pictures glorifying the Roman noble families. On the other side of the coins they had portraits of famous living people. The first of these was Julius Caesar.

To pay debts incurred in their many wars the Romans, following the example of Athens some three hundred years earlier, reduced the metal content of the coins, making them lighter, although the face value remained the same. The government kept the metals saved in this way to meet its debts.

Following the Roman victory over Carthage the money remained stable for a long period but the country's finances again ran into difficulties when successive emperors lavished money gifts on their favourite Romans. Nero started a new series of coin debasements which lasted until the end of the third century. He not only reduced the metals in the coins but also issued coins made from base metals with a gold or silver coating. This debasement reached a point when the people refused to accept coins at their face value and the money system was in danger of collapsing altogether. The government then introduced reforms to stabilise the currency and it remained so until the break-up of the Roman Empire.

2 Pounds, Shillings and Pence

THE earliest currency to circulate in Britain was in the form of iron bars, crudely made and of varying sizes. A large number of these bars, rather like half-finished swords, has been discovered in the Midlands and the South West. Some authorities believe that they actually were swords left by their makers before they were completed, but it is now generally accepted that they were examples of the many 'tool' currencies that circulated in Europe at the time. In the south gold coins that came from Gaul (northern France) circulated with the iron bars but, as communications were difficult in those days, they never reached the northern part of the country.

When the Romans arrived in Britain in 55 BC they found the iron bars still in existence but most of the tribes were also using their own rough coins. These early native coins were very crude copper or tin castings made in clay and wooden moulds. We think the Ancient Britons learned how to mint coins from western Europeans who came over to the country about that time.

The Romans soon introduced their own coins and the tribal coins went out of existence. The first coins came from Rome but, from the third century AD, the Romans minted them in London.

After the Romans left in AD 414 the coinage system became confused. Local Anglo-Saxon rulers minted coins of their own

Early British coins: 1 gold solidus of Roman Britain, Magnus Maximus 4th century A D; 2 silver penny of Anglo Saxon period, Offa of Mercia 8th century A D; 3 silver penny thought to be of William I 1066-87; 4 silver groat thought to be of Edward I 1272-1307; 5 gold sovereign, second issue 1526-43, of Henry VIII; 6 silver half-crown 1551 of Edward VI; 7 silver sixpence of Elizabeth I 1558-1603; 8 copper farthing, second issue 1604-25, of James I (James VI of Scotland)

design and this resulted in a mass of small crude silver coins of different types. The silver penny was first issued during the reign of Offa of Mercia, about AD 760. The name was probably derived from *pening*, *penig* or *pending*, from an old German word meaning 'a pledge or value'. The standard was 240 pennies from one pound weight of silver. Also in the Saxon era a coin called a *scilling* (meaning 'a division') appeared and this coin was originally worth four silver pennies.

Following the Norman Invasion in 1066 William the Conqueror continued to mint the Saxon pennies. He built his mint in the Tower of London and introduced a new silver standard, known as 'sterling silver', which had 925 parts of pure silver in every 1,000. Except for a few departures, such as that of Henry VIII, sterling silver was the rule from the Conquest until 1920, and those who deviated were forced by public opinion to return to the standard which was regarded as 'ancient and right'.

The silver penny was the only coin that circulated in Britain until towards the end of the thirteenth century. But the Normans adopted the Roman system of keeping accounts. The system was based on three different values. The *libra* (one pound weight of silver) was equal to twenty *solidi*, and the *solidus* was worth twelve *denarii* (pennies). Later the Saxon *scilling* replaced the Roman *solidus*. This is the origin of the British 'pounds, shillings and pence' and the signs '£' (*libra*), 's' (*solidi*) and 'd' (*denarii*).

Prices were quoted in pennies, shillings and pounds. When the price of an article reached 240 pennies it was said to be a pound—from the pound weight of silver—although the pound *as a coin* did not appear until the reign of Henry VII, almost two centuries later. Similarly, at the lower end, if something was priced at twelve pennies, it was worth a shilling, although the shilling coin only came into existence, like the pound, at the time of Henry VII. In Saxon times the value of the shilling was four or five pennies but, when William of Normandy came to the throne, he established the value of the Norman shilling at twelve pennies. So it has remained until the present-day change to decimal currency.

As more silver pennies were minted their appearance improved.

The lettering and impressions became clearer but the drawback was the smooth edge. It was easy for unscrupulous people to steal a little of the silver by filing the edge and restoring the smooth surface. The thieves who did this became expert and it was difficult to detect a clipped coin until it had been noticeably reduced in size. This evil practice continued until the end of the seventeenth century, when a Frenchman, Pierre Blondeau, invented a machine to manufacture coins with milled edges.

Clipping was not the only problem. Another menace from early times and through the Middle Ages was counterfeiting. It was easy and profitable to make imitations of the official coins in baser metals and, although those found guilty of this crime were severely punished, a steady flow of forged money circulated with the good money.

The number of clipped and counterfeit coins in circulation became so great at times that the value of the currency fell far below the legal standard and the authorities were forced to take action. They would then call in *all* the coins and reissue new ones of standard weight and fineness. The authorities refused to stand the loss incurred in this operation and so it fell on the shoulders of those unfortunate people who held the bad money because they received fewer standard coins in exchange for the bad coins they were forced to hand in. To mitigate this loss the authorities sometimes minted coins of the same metal but lighter in weight. This went on for many years until, at the end of the fifteenth century, they were making 480 pennies, instead of 240, from one pound weight of silver.

A penny was still a penny for the purpose of buying goods, ie it retained the same purchasing power, but the amount of silver in the coin had been reduced by one half. Money, as a means of buying things, now appeared to exist separately from the metals used to make the coins.

From about the middle of the thirteenth century more coins were added to the currency. In 1257, Henry III issued a gold penny, worth twenty silver pennies, but this coin did not prove popular. Nearly ninety years were to elapse before gold coins appeared again. In 1279, Edward I introduced silver half-pence

English gold coins: 1 penny, Henry III; 2 noble, Edward III; 3 angel, Henry VI; 4 sovereign, Henry VII; 5 guinea, Charles II

and farthings to replace the pennies cut into halves and quarters to meet the people's need for coins of lower value.

At this time the inelasticity of the single coin system was becoming apparent and there was also a need for a coin larger than a penny. To meet this requirement the authorities minted the groat, which was worth four pennies, but, like the earlier gold penny, this coin did not prove as popular as expected.

Almost a century after the appearance of the unpopular gold penny a second gold coin was minted. This was the florin, issued in 1344, and valued at six shillings. The people liked it no better than the gold penny and it was withdrawn within a few months. Nevertheless the need for gold currency persisted, especially among the wealthier people, and later in the same year the gold noble was minted. The value was 6s 8d, which was one-third of a pound weight of silver. The noble, so-called because gold was looked on as a noble metal, was accepted by the people and followed by the half-noble and the quarter-noble.

By the middle of the fourteenth century gold nobles, half-nobles, quarter-nobles, silver groats, half-groats, half-pennies and farthings had been added to the silver penny and remained in circulation for eighty years. Further gold coins were minted during the reigns of Henry VI and Edward IV. These were the angel, half-angel and rose-noble.

In addition to minting the first gold sovereign Henry VII introduced the silver shilling and this coin, with varying metal content, has remained in circulation until the present day. Probably the most famous shilling was the 'lion' shilling, which bore the Royal Crest of a lion, and which first appeared during the reign of George IV. In the following years these coins disappeared from circulation but were minted again after the coronation of Edward VII. During the reigns of Henry VII and Henry VIII shillings were minted from fine silver but gradually the silver content was reduced by using base metals. The silver— or part-silver shilling—was replaced in 1946 by a shilling made of cupro-nickel and the cupro-nickel shilling has been retained as the 5-pence piece in the decimal currency system.

Britain owes the crown and half-crown coins to Henry VIII.

His crown coin was made of gold but crowns minted during the reign of his son, Edward VI, were of gold and silver. By the time Charles II came to the throne in 1649 all the crowns were made of silver. The first silver crown was a famous and impressive coin depicting Edward VI on horseback and bearing the date 1551. This was the first time a date appeared on a coin. Crowns of varying design have continued to be minted since 1551 and the four hundredth anniversary of the first crown was celebrated by the minting of two million cupro-nickel crowns during the 1951 Festival of Britain.

During his short reign Edward VI contributed the small silver coins—the sixpence and threepenny pieces. For some time before this sixpences of base metal had been in circulation and, because of their poor quality, people gave them slang names like 'bender' and 'tanner'. The coin was called 'bender' because it could be doubled in the fingers and the name 'tanner' has remained to this day.

The silver half-pence and farthings introduced by Edward I towards the end of the thirteenth century lasted almost two hundred years and, when they disappeared, shopkeepers and other traders made tokens of lead and tin to take their place. James I disliked the token coins and in 1613 decided to stop the shopkeepers from using them. He authorised the mint to strike copper farthings in his name and, in 1672, government copper coins came into being by the regular issue of half-pennies and farthings. In 1860 bronze replaced copper and has been used for this purpose ever since. Another important change also took place in the same year. The design was changed from the 'young head' to the 'bun head' because of Queen Victoria's hair style and this change throws an interesting light on the Queen's attitude towards the designs. With the exception of the 'old head' coins minted between 1895 and 1901 the portrait was always of her in her much younger days.

Owing to the activities of the clippers the silver penny, still the most important coin at that time, weighed only eight grains when Elizabeth I ascended the throne in 1558. At the end of the seventeenth century, when it was considered too light and small

29

English coins: 1 copper twopence 1797 of George III; 2 silver shilling ('Lion Shilling') 1826 of George IV; 3 copper penny ('Bun Penny') 1881 of Victoria; 4 silver florin 1893 of Victoria; 5 cupro-nickel crown 1953 of Elizabeth II, obverse showing the Queen habited as Colonel-in-Chief Grenadier Guards; 6 cupro-nickel crown 1965 struck in honour of Sir Winston Churchill, the reverse, showing Sir Winston, designed by Oscar Nemon

to be of any further service to the people, Charles II decided to discontinue its issue. So ended, after almost a thousand years, what was probably the most important coin in the British system. Charles II minted a few copper half-pence but they were never used. Copper pence did not come into circulation until the time of George III, a century later. These were the penny and two-penny pieces, which weighed one ounce and two ounces. They were thick and cumbersome and people found them inconvenient to carry in their pockets and purses.

It has been said that Charles II contributed more to the history of the British coinage than any other monarch. He was responsible for bringing to an end the centuries-old silver penny and he minted the first copper coin. He introduced the machine that made coins with milled edges and it was he who had the figure of Britannia impressed on the coins. His head on the coins faced in the opposite direction to that of previous monarchs and it is said that he did this because he was ashamed of his father, Charles I, who was beheaded.

Although Britain had the short-lived gold florin in the fourteenth century, five hundred years were to elapse before the silver florin or two-shilling piece made its appearance. Called a 'florin' from *Florentia*, the Latin name for the city of Florence, this coin has proved very popular for over a hundred years and is still used as the 10-penny piece in the new decimal system.

Although the pound had been used to measure value and to keep accounts for centuries, the pound *coin*, called a sovereign, did not appear until about the year 1500. It was called a sovereign because the first gold coin bore the picture of King Henry VII sitting on the throne wearing his crown and mantle and holding his sceptre and orb. The sovereign was minted until the outbreak of the 1914-18 war, when it was withdrawn and replaced by £1 Treasury notes.

Although the gold sovereign was in circulation, Britain continued to value things in terms of silver for over three hundred years. It was not until 1817 that she changed from the 'silver standard' to the 'gold standard' and measured values in terms of the sovereign. In that year half-sovereigns were minted; they

31

were made from eleven parts pure gold and one part copper to render them more hard-wearing.

For about a hundred years from the accession of Queen Victoria £5 gold pieces were minted, but these coins were not very popular even among wealthy people. The golden guinea, worth twenty-one shillings, and so-called because it was minted from gold from the Guinea Coast of Africa, came into circulation about the middle of the seventeenth century and lasted some two hundred years. Although it is no longer used in Britain, club and other subscriptions are still quoted in guineas and bids are made in guineas at Tattersall's Racehorse Auctions and at Christie's and Sotheby's, where paintings and art objects are sold.

Although no longer used in Britain the gold sovereign has lost none of its popularity in some other countries, where there is a continuing demand for this coin which, if the supply is insufficient, leads to counterfeiting. To meet this demand the Royal Mint exported over 4,700 million sovereigns in 1968. Gold coins are issued by some countries to commemorate historical events and happenings. To mark the second anniversary of her secession from the Nigerian Federation Biafra issued 3,000 sets of gold coins in five denominations, from £25 to £1. They were offered for sale to collectors in Switzerland at a price of £195 a set.

Before we leave the British coinage we should mention the fact that dollars were once used in its currency. In the early eighteenth century, during the reign of George III, there was an acute shortage of silver to mint the coins. To bridge the gap a supply of silver pieces-of-eight (equalling eight reals), which they called dollars, was obtained from Spain. To mark them for special use in Britain they were impressed with the king's head. The Spanish dollars were taken across the Atlantic to the Spanish-American colonies and in course of time they became the basis of the American currency.

In Scotland the coinage system has broadly kept in step with the English system but the Scots from time to time added a few coins of their own. About the year 1550, during the reign of Mary, Queen of Scots, they minted a coin called a testoon, worth four to five shillings in English money, and the mark, valued at thirteen

Scottish and Irish coins. Scottish: 1 gold St Andrew or Lion (current for 5s) of Robert III 1390-1406; 2 billion 'bawbee', derived from 'bas billon', or plack (current for 1¹/₂d) of James V 1514-42; 3 silver testoon 1553 (current for 4s) of Mary Queen of Scots. Irish: 4 Dublin silver penny of Aethelred II 979-1016; 5 silver groat 1556 (current for one third of a shilling) of Philip and Mary; 6 copper crown 1690 ('Gun Money') of James II

shillings in Scotland but worth about three shillings in English money. The well-known 'bawbee' appeared about this time. Valued originally at a penny half-penny it rose to sixpence. During their reigns Mary and James V also struck gold coins.

During the reign of James VI (James I of England) the Scots issued a variety of coins. There was a twenty-pound gold piece, a four-pound piece called a ducat, a sword, a thistle merk and others for circulation in Scotland. In earlier times they had the St Andrew, or lion, the demy-lion or demy, the rider, half-rider and quarter-rider, unicorn and half-unicorn, and bonnet piece. The last coins to be struck in Scotland were the series issued during the time of Queen Anne, in the early eighteenth century, which included a silver ten-shilling piece.

Irish coins originated from the time the Danes ruled England. Coins bearing the name of Aethelred II (Ethelred the Unready) were used in Ireland in the early eleventh century but it is not certain whether these coins were actually made in England or whether they were imitations made by local Irish rulers.

Prince John, son of Henry II, who was the Lord of Ireland, struck the first English coins in Ireland at the end of the twelfth century. They were the farthing, the half-penny and later the penny. Little is known about the coinage history of Ireland for the next three centuries but, towards the end of the fifteenth century, Lambert Simnel, who was crowned Edward VI in Dublin, issued groats and pennies.

At the end of the seventeenth century, during the reign of James II, a crown, half-crown and a shilling, made of gun metal, a pewter penny and a brass half-penny were in circulation. By the early nineteenth century the Irish had ceased to mint their own coins and used English coins until 1928, when the Republic of Ireland came into being. The coins that circulated in the Republic were silver half-crowns, shillings and sixpences, nickel three-penny pieces and bronze pennies and half-pennies. In February 1971 the Republic of Eire adopted the same decimal currency system as the United Kingdom.

On 15 February 1971 the Act passed by Parliament in 1967 was implemented and Great Britain changed to decimal currency.

There is no change in the banknotes, except that the 10 shilling note has been discarded. The pound, formerly divided into 20 shillings and 240 pence, is now made up of 100 pence. A new 50-penny piece has replaced the old 10s note and is worth exactly the same. The old 2s piece remains but it is now valued at 10 new pence. There is also a new 10-pence piece of the same size. The shilling piece has been retained but its value is now 5 new pence. As a temporary measure the sixpence, threepenny bit and the old penny continued to be used but the last two had to be tendered in units of sixpence or one shilling. On 31 August 1971 the three-penny piece and the penny were withdrawn from circulation.

The Decimal Currency Board gave the following reasons for the change in the British coinage: (a) the new system is easier than the old one based on 20 shillings and 240 pence to the pound, (b) it is more efficient for business, and (c) it is already used in almost every country in the world, so trade and travel will be simpler.

The decimal system was known in Europe in the Middle Ages and recommendations for decimal coinage go back to the sixteenth century and probably earlier. With a desire for simplicity the United States adopted decimal currency in 1792 and France did so in the following year. From 1841 to 1963 various Royal Commissions and Committees in Britain considered the desir-ability of changing the coinage but the problem facing all these bodies was how to adopt the pound sterling of 240 pennies to decimals. There was strong opposition to abandoning the pound as the unit of currency. It was feared that such action would endanger the position of London as a centre of international trade and finance.

The 1967 Act was a compromise. The pound was retained as the basic unit but divided into 100 new pence, each equal to 2·4 old pennies. The new 10p and 5p pieces will eventually replace the florin and the shilling, the latter having been in use since Anglo-Saxon times.

1773354

3 The Dollar Story

WHEN the first European settlers arrived in the New World during the sixteenth century they found the Indians using as money strings of shell beads, known as wampum. The colonists first traded goods with the Indians but later they also adopted wampum as their money and, from that time, wampum played a vital part in the growth of trade and commerce in the northern part of the continent. The value of wampum, like that of the cowrie shells of the Pacific, varied with the length of the beads.

The Indians patiently and laboriously drilled holes in the shells with their primitive tools but, by using lathes and drills, the settlers cut the work down to a fraction of the time and supplies of wampum became so plentiful that it lost its scarcity value and ceased to act as money. When wampum was of no further use the settlers reverted to barter by exchanging goods, such as corn, sugar, tobacco, rum, cotton, molasses, and even tomahawk pipes like the one illustrated.

By this time the Spanish dollars or pieces-of-eight, which had come from Europe to the Spanish-American colonies, trickled through from Mexico to the western part of the country and then to the eastern states. The dollar (valued at eight reals) was a large silver coin too valuable for small purchases and the colonists

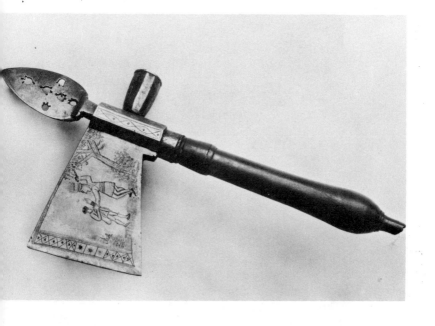

Tomahawk pipe, from the Eastern Woodlands Indians of North America, with native engraving. These weapons were traded by the white settlers to the Indians

met their everyday needs by paying with sugar and tobacco.

Realising that a purely barter system was inconvenient the colonists gave some of their commodities a fixed price in money terms so that the goods could actually be used as money. Tobacco was the first item selected and in course of time became the only legal currency.

Tobacco would buy everything. A writer of the time records that, as soon as an immigrant ship was approaching the harbour, you could see the young men of Virginia rushing to the waterfront with bundles of tobacco in their arms. With the tobacco they paid the passages of their wives or sweethearts from the old country. The fare was usually 100 lb of tobacco, which was worth between £10 and £15.

Events proved that the choice of tobacco as a currency was a

North American wampum belt. Wampum was used by the Indians and early colonists for primitive barter until it was made so plentiful that it lost its value

mistake. In 1619 the authorities fixed a price of between one shilling and sixpence and three shillings a pound according to quality. In the next ten years the average price rose to three shillings and sixpence a pound. Attracted by the rising price the growers increased their efforts and, within three years, there was so much tobacco that the price fell to sixpence a pound. Like the wampum, tobacco was no longer a good currency because it had ceased to be scarce.

The authorities tried to control the amount of tobacco grown and to improve the quality. They limited the number of plants and would not allow people to grow it in their spare time. This had no effect. Prices continued to fall and, within the next ten years, tobacco was threepence a pound. By 1665 it was a penny a pound. In 1666 the authorities repealed the law making tobacco legal currency but people continued to use it to pay for the ordinary things of life. The few Spanish reals that were about could only be used to make large purchases.

The colonists tried in vain to have the authorities ban the growing of tobacco for a year so as to increase the price. They took the law into their own hands, banded together and destroyed the crops. Things became so bad that those who were caught were sentenced to death.

The authorities next issued what came to be known as 'tobacco notes', which were made legal tender in 1727. These notes of different denominations depicted a tobacco leaf or marks of particular brands of tobacco. They can still be seen at some museums in the southern States.

About the turn of the eighteenth century people in South Carolina used rice to pay their taxes. Shortly afterwards the authorities issued rice orders or rice-notes. For every 100 lb of rice handed in the people received a note to the value of 2s 6d. It was much easier to buy what they wanted with the notes than with the rice itself and they used the notes to make every kind of purchase. The authorities were determined to keep up the value of the notes and anyone found forging them was sentenced to death.

At this time money was in a disorganised state all over the

Coins produced in 1652 by the first mint set up by the colonists in Boston: 1 oak tree sixpence; 2 pine tree shilling

world and in many countries men were trying to adapt a currency system based on some staple product or products. In the West Indies the people conducted their business in sugar, which had a fixed price of 10s for 100 lb. They used sugar for all transactions—even to pay small fines.

The American colonists appealed to the British Treasury for a supply of coins but the Treasury refused their request. Some resourceful colonists then showed their initiative by minting their own coins. They set up their first mint in Boston and, in 1652, they produced shillings, sixpences and threepenny pieces bearing different designs, such as pine, willow and oak trees. At this time Lord Baltimore, realising the colonists' predicament, had some shillings, sixpences, groats and copper pennies specially minted in England and shipped to Maryland.

Although some coins circulated in certain areas the people still used goods as currency. In Canada, furs and grain were legally used as money but no doubt the most curious money ever to circulate in that country was the Card money, first issued in 1685, which lasted until the eighteenth century. The authorities made this money from ordinary playing cards and, within a hundred years, Card money for a total of a million French livres was in circulation.

This Card money had a curious origin. The French representative in Canada found himself short of money as that due to him from France had not arrived. He needed funds desperately to pay his soldiers. He was a resourceful man and, as he had no paper or presses to print paper money, he decided to use playing cards. He collected all the cards he could find and cut them into quarters. On some of the segments he inserted 'four francs', on others 'forty sols' and on the remainder 'fifteen sols'. With these three denominations he could pay exact amounts from large to small. He signed all the cards himself. The representative had brought into use an excellent type of paper money. It was hard-wearing, difficult to forge and—as it turned out—willingly accepted by everybody.

About five years afterwards he made a further issue because the money that France sent to him had been lost at sea. The people continued to accept this strange money and more issues were made. This arrangement went on for years. It suited the King of France because it relieved him of the burden of sending coins to Canada frequently with the risk of capture or shipwreck. It had another advantage too. While the people in Canada used the Card money they remained loyal to the French King. If they turned against him he would refuse to send shipments of coin to Canada and their chances of redeeming their pieces of playing card were gone.

When the Card money was circulating in Canada many American States were minting their own coins. The first one seen was probably the Massachusetts pine tree shilling, which appeared in 1652. At first all those states which had mints issued only silver coins but in 1785 Vermont and Connecticut produced copper cents. This was the beginning of the dollar and cent system in the United States. In the new country the emphasis was on simplicity, which led to the early adoption of the metric system. In 1792 a mint was set up in Philadelphia which produced large quantities of dimes, worth one-tenth of a dollar, and half dimes, with the American eagle on one side and the head of Liberty on the other.

The coins were made from scrap copper collected from all over the country and some three hundred different types of coins were

*Five-cent piece of 1915 (first issued in 1913), known as
the Buffalo, Bison or Indian head nickel*

produced up to 1815, when metals became short during the wars with England. The early copper coins ceased, to be followed later by the famous Indian chief and buffalo half-dimes and five cent coins or nickels.

The Philadelphia mint was a somewhat primitive building where the work was done by hand and the rollers pulled by horses. A new mint, larger and more modern, was opened in 1833.

The word 'dollar' is not of American origin. It was originally 'thaler', a shortened version of 'Joachimsthaler', a coin minted from silver mined in Joachim's Dale, in Bohemia, Germany. As with many continental words the English found the word 'thaler' difficult to pronounce and in course of time it changed to the simpler word 'dollar'.

One of the earliest references to the dollar in English literature was in Shakespeare's *Macbeth*, where Ross tells Malcolm of the Norsemen who had been killed but were denied burial until their king had disbursed 'ten thousand dollars to our general use'.

The coin was first minted in the sixteenth century and within

*Model of the first coining press at the Philadelphia Mint,
late 18th century*

a few years it became so popular that it was used in many
European countries. In the book *Travels* written by an English-
man named Sandys, which appeared about the year 1610, it is
said that the word was already in use in three continents, Europe,
Africa and Asia. The author relates that he hired a boat in Egypt
for twelve dollars and says that Dutch dollars circulated in
Phoenicia on a par with Spanish pieces-of-eight. He also mentions
that he found a monastery on Mount Sinai to be 'receiving an
annual revenue of 60,000 dollars from Christian princes'.

In 1642 the colony of Massachusetts recognised the Rix dollar,
a corruption of 'Reichsthaler' used by the German immigrants,
and valued it at five shillings. The thaler was the coin of the
German Empire and it was under the rule of Charles V, Emperor
of Germany, King of Spain and Lord of Spanish America, that

German thalers and Spanish pieces-of-eight became the chief coin in the old world and the new world respectively. The Spanish pieces-of-eight flowed into the new world from southern Europe and the West Indies.

As time went on these Spanish dollars crossed the Atlantic and were used in the Spanish-American colonies. During the next three hundred years most of the world's trade was financed by these coins and they were seen in thousands not only in America and Europe but in Africa, the West Indies and as far away as Australia. We are all familiar with the Spanish pieces-of-eight, having read about them in stirring stories of buried treasure and pirate adventure all over the seas.

Arising mainly from the numerous revolutions in Spanish America the Spanish and Mexican dollars grew fewer and fewer and finally disappeared, to be replaced centuries later by the dollar minted in the United States.

Early American dollar, 1794: obverse, head of Liberty with fifteen stars representing the number of States in the Union at the time; reverse, American eagle with spread wings standing on palm branches

The first American dollar was minted towards the end of the eighteenth century. It was a fine silver coin bearing on one side the head of Liberty, with thirteen stars representing the original states of the Union. On the reverse side there was the American eagle with wings outstretched. In 1921 they issued the 'Peace Dollar' with all details the same as the original dollar except that the eagle's wings were folded. The word 'Peace' was under the eagle's claws, which held an olive branch. Perhaps the eagle looked less war-like and more in keeping with peace than with its wings stretched out.

There have been many theories as to the origin of the symbol $ prefixing the American currency. It was once thought that it was a modification of the English £ sign, but this is considered unlikely. Other theories were that it derived from a roughly written US—the initials of the United States—or that it related to the figure 8, indicating the Spanish coin of eight reals or pieces-of-eight. Other suppositions, now dismissed, were that the sign came from the Roman money units, the sesterces, denoted by the mark HS (which could be easily changed to the dollar sign); or from the Spanish contraction for *peso*, a dollar, indicated by combining the letters P and S; or again from the Spanish word *fuertes*, meaning hard, and used to distinguish coin from paper money.

The theory now accepted is that the sign derives from the twin

Spanish dollar or piece of eight (valued at eight reals) of Philip V of Spain. It retained the emblem of Charles V of two pillars entwined with scrolls and was still known as the 'Pillar Piece'

45

pillars of early times connected as religious emblems by the Phoenicians and denoting strength and sovereignty.

The twin pillars originate from Solomon's temple. When Tyrian workmen built the temple they erected with great ceremony at the front of the porch two pillars of brass, one named Jachin, or 'He shall establish', and the other, Boaz, or, 'In it is strength'.

Ancient Tyrian coins bore the symbolic pillars and there is a tradition that a Tyrian explorer named Melcanthus, sailing through the Straits of Gibraltar, placed the Tyrian symbols of sovereignty on a site that is now Cadiz. Over the pillars he built a temple to the Phoenician god Heracles, afterwards known as Hercules. The colony grew in wealth and power and the Pillars of Hercules, said to be 'the chains that bind together the earth and the sea', became the colony's emblem.

The Spanish interests of Emperor Charles V of Germany led him to incorporate the arms of the Holy Roman Empire with the Spanish arms, and the standard dollar, minted in Seville and known as the 'Pillar Piece', had as an emblem these two pillars entwined with a scroll. It was thought that this represented the serpents sent by Juno to destroy the infant Hercules, but in reality it was a revival of the old Tyrian custom. The pillar pieces of Charles V restored to the world's notice the symbols borne by the Tyrian coins many centuries earlier.

The dollar sign was first a religious emblem and then a symbol of authority and, through the ancient Tyrian coinage and Spanish domination, came to bear its present significance.

4 Paper Money

THE Chinese invented paper money as long ago as 2697 BC. It was printed in blue ink on paper made from the fibre of the mulberry tree, and the Chinese called it 'flying money' because, unlike the heavy metals in use, it flew with the wind. Some of this 'flying money' still exists. Carefully preserved in the Asiatic Museum, Leningrad, is a note printed in 1339 BC while in the British Museum there are others dating from the 14th century BC during the time of the Ming Dynasty.

The Chinese also made notes from parchment and this once led to the extinction of a lovely breed of deer. The notes, measuring a Chinese foot square, were called 'skin notes' and were parts of the skin of a white stag. Each note was worth forty thousand chuen. To keep up the value of the notes by limiting the supply of skins the Chinese restricted the number of white deer and as a result the beautiful deer became extinct and forever lost to the world.

More than 4,000 years later in 1661, the first European bank note appeared in Sweden, and before the end of the seventeenth century bank notes were being printed and issued in England.

London goldsmiths originated the bank note when they began to act as bankers as well as carrying out their own trade. People deposited money with them for safe keeping in their strong-

*No specimen of the first European bank note, issued in
Sweden in 1661, is extant. This is the Swedish bank note
(or note of credit) of 1662*

rooms, and the goldsmiths gave them a receipt for it. These
receipts took the form of a promise to repay the person who had
lodged the money but, by 1670, the words 'or bearer' had been
added after the name of the depositor. This meant that the goldsmith would hand over the money to the depositor or to the
person who was the bearer of the note—the person in whose
possession it was when it was presented. Knowing for certain
that the notes would be fully redeemed when they were presented
people passed them from hand to hand as a substitute for money.

In 1694 the Bank of England was founded and the issue of
notes was its most important function. While some small banks

still continued to issue their own notes, by 1750 the Bank of England note was the most important form of paper money in the country.

Until the end of the eighteenth century people could present bank notes at the Bank of England and demand payment in gold. But the threat of invasion by Napoleon in 1797 caused them to panic and they swarmed into the Bank with their notes. Fearing a run on the stocks of gold Parliament ordered the Bank to suspend payment and this suspension continued throughout the Napoleonic War. The Bank increased the issue of notes during the War, but the amount never exceeded the reserve of gold that it held. Although prices almost doubled in the war years the people never again lost confidence in the notes and transactions were conducted as if they had been golden sovereigns.

In 1821, the Bank paid the notes again in gold and, between then and 1840, there were several severe financial crises and many believed that the cause was the large volume of notes in circulation following the end of the War. In 1844, one hundred and fifty years after it was formed, the Bank of England Charter was renewed. This led to the passing of the famous Bank Charter Act which stabilised and governed our currency until 1914.

The Act divided the Bank of England into two Departments—the Issue Department and the Banking Department. The Issue Department's sole function was to issue notes. It issued notes backed pound for pound by the gold and silver it held in the vaults and, in addition, it was allowed by Parliament to issue a further £14 million, called the Fiduciary Issue, which was covered by government securities alone.

The Act also prohibited any new bank from issuing notes and those banks that were already printing their own private notes were not allowed to increase them. By the year 1921 the Bank of England had the monopoly of note issue in England and Wales but the Scottish banks and the banks in Northern Ireland continue to issue their own notes in denominations of £1, £5, £10, £20, £50 and £100.

Because they were forbidden to issue notes the other banks developed a means of transferring money by another form of

D

paper and brought the cheque into use. At the time the Italians and the Dutch used cheques but they did not originate in these countries. The credit again goes to the goldsmiths. When the goldsmith bankers started business towards the middle of the seventeenth century they kept what they called 'running cashes', which later became known as current accounts. Customers paid cash and cheques into these accounts and transferred money to other people by issuing a cheque instructing the banker to transfer a stated sum of money to the person named in the cheque. For a long time this keeping of current accounts and issuing cheques against the balance was confined to London, but in the nineteenth century it spread rapidly to the provinces.

The First World War marked the beginning of a revolution in the money system. The gold sovereigns and half-sovereigns were called in and replaced by £1 and 10s Treasury Notes. From 1914 to 1925 the notes could not be converted into gold and, during the period 1925 until 1931, they were convertible only if the presenter accepted a minimum of 400 ounce bars of gold, costing £1,500. It was obvious that few people could take advantage of this arrangement.

In 1931 Britain abandoned the Gold Standard and all notes in circulation were no longer convertible. Although the notes were not backed by gold and silver people still had confidence in them and continued to buy goods with them as they had done before.

The issue of notes unbacked by gold increased as time went on to meet the needs of trade and business. In 1954 it was £1,600 million and in 1963 it had increased to £2,600 million. It now stands at about £3,500 million.

At the outbreak of the Second World War in 1939 all the Bank's stock of gold was transferred to pay for food and munitions imported from abroad and *all* the notes now circulating are completely without backing by any precious metals.

When the banks were printing their own private notes there were many that bore attractive designs, but perhaps some of the most interesting of bank notes ever seen in Britain were those printed by the Bank of the Black Sheep—as it came to be known —in west Wales. The Bank issued notes for £1, £2 and 10s. On

Welsh pound note of 1813 issued by the Aberystwyth &
Tregaron Bank, known as the Bank of the Black Sheep
because of its sheep emblems: the £2 note had two ewes,
and the 10s note had a lamb

the £1 note there was the picture of one black ewe, the £2 note
bore two black ewes and a black lamb was portrayed on the 10s
note. Most of the folk who handled the notes were illiterate, and
this enabled them to tell the difference in value.

The recent revival of this Bank's name in the modern title of
The Black Sheep Company of Wales Limited (Cwmni y Ddafad
Ddu Cymreig Limited) has been publicised by the press and
television. In addition to the £1, £2 and 10s notes, notes of £5 and
£10 have been issued. To distinguish them from the lower values
the £5 note has a picture of one black *ram* and the £10 note has
two black rams. The sheep motif, while no longer necessary to
indicate the note value, has been retained as a continuance of the
original design.

Following the disappearance of the silver dollar in the United
States paper money came more and more into use and nowadays
the Americans use it exclusively except for small change. Great
Britain and other European countries use less paper money
because they have more *coins* of higher value in circulation. For
example, Great Britain now has a coin worth 50 new pence, about

10s, whereas the largest American coin is the quarter, worth 20 cents—roughly 10 new pence in English money.

Before the revolt of the American colonists against British rule in 1775 all the colonies issued their own paper dollars. When the fighting started in the same year with the Battle of Lexington, Congress decided to issue official paper money. Soon over two million dollars worth of paper was in circulation and within the next four years this had risen to two hundred and forty million dollars.

Unlike the government of Britain, which has maintained rigid control over the country's paper money, Congress failed to take this precaution. Soon there were so many paper dollars in circulation that the value of the dollar, nominally 100 silver cents, had dropped to three cents. By the year 1780 you would have had to give forty paper dollars for one silver one. Prices rose beyond control. People had to pay five thousand paper dollars for a pair of shoes. Barbers papered their saloons with the worthless money and the story goes that sailors paraded the streets in gay suits made of the paper money they received as wages. Hundreds of thousands of thrifty people, who had saved their paper dollars in good faith, were ruined.

At this time a financial expert named Robert Morris made an appearance. He established the first national bank—the Bank of North America—which issued notes that the people could trust. Their trust was not misplaced. The dollar retained its par value of 100 silver cents and for the next thirty years there followed a period of reliable currency and steady prices.

In 1812 war broke out between the United States and Britain. This brought on money troubles more serious than the people had ever experienced before. Taking advantage of the earlier stable conditions hundreds of small banks had sprung up all over the country. They all issued their own notes but there were also many forged notes around. People would not accept new notes because they thought they were forged. They preferred old and dirty ones or those with pin-holes, which showed that they had passed through many banks. By 1861, when the American Civil War broke out, there were seven thousand different kinds of paper

Henry Ford with the ten millionth Model 'T' (the 'Tin Lizzie') and the first car he built, the Quadricycle

money in circulation. There were also five thousand varieties of forged notes.

The Americans had a grim struggle to bring the value of the paper dollar to its present level, when it is accepted without question in any part of the world. Beginning at the end of the Civil War their effort lasted for almost a century. Slowly but surely an improvement came about as the country's prosperity increased. Perhaps the United States more than any other country owes its wealth and prestige to the efforts of individuals—men like John D. Rockefeller, J. Pierpoint Morgan, Andrew Carnegie, Harriman the railway king, F. W. Woolworth and Henry Ford.

John D. Rockefeller, who started life as a farm labourer, organised and controlled the gigantic business that developed from the discovery of oil in America about the middle of the nineteenth century. His fortune has been estimated at about two thousand million dollars and he gave away almost half of it during his lifetime.

J. Pierpoint Morgan was a financial genius who also helped to increase America's prosperity. In 1915 his banking company, Morgan & Company, negotiated a loan to Britain of five hundred million dollars, which was the largest in the world up to that time. Morgan's agents spent the money in the United States purchasing essential war materials without which Britain could not continue the war. This was some three years before America actively entered the war by sending troops to Europe. The dollar was so powerful at this stage that it can be said that with this act financial control of much of the world passed from British to American hands.

The American steel industry was developed by Andrew Carnegie, who endowed libraries all over the world from his personal fortune of four hundred million dollars. The Harriman family controlled the railways and the tobacco industry owes much of its existence to a magnate named 'Buck' Duke. F. W. Woolworth founded the 'five and ten' store in 1879 where all the goods were priced at 5 cents or 10 cents. His branch shops are now to be found in most of the civilised parts of the world.

Perhaps the greatest contribution to America's amazing

William Morris (later Lord Nuffield) with the 1923 Cowley 2-seater

prosperity was made by Henry Ford. He started the mass production of motor cars by introducing the moving-belt system with one workman doing one job only on the car as the belt moved endlessly along. He produced the first people's car—the Model 'T' Ford—which came to be known as the 'Tin Lizzie'. He manufactured hundreds of thousands of these cars, which were used by people in America, Britain and Europe who had never been able to afford a car before. The model was cheap to buy and to run.

Soon the mass-production of cars spread to other countries and, in a short time, Britain had its cheap people's cars to rival the Ford. These were the early Morris cars—including the famous 'Bull-nose'—produced in Oxford by a pioneer named William Morris, who later became Lord Nuffield. He donated the greater part of his large personal fortune to charity.

Henry Ford said that the motor car would revolutionise society. The revolution became more far-reaching than anyone could foresee at the time. In addition to congestion on the roads and in the towns the motor car is responsible for the menace of air pollution from millions of exhausts. This pollution is becoming a major problem in all the world's largest cities.

To overcome this hazard to health experiments are now being carried out in America to devise some alternative means of propulsion. It is interesting to note that in the van of these new developments is the Ford Foundation, which is financing research into the possibilities of bringing back the old steam-driven car. Thus the Ford empire, which has accumulated its wealth from the profits made on petrol-driven cars, is using this wealth to lessen the nuisance created in a large degree by its own product. If the 'steamer' or the electric car ever again become practical propositions it is probable that the Ford organisation with its foresight and drive will seize the opportunity to amass further wealth.

Consumer goods produced on the conveyor-belt system became plentiful in America, then in Britain, and later, in many other countries. Production has now reached such a level in America that there is a danger of people becoming overburdened with consumer goods and regarding them as a nuisance. It is no longer fashionable to keep your car, fridge, television set, washing machine or vacuum cleaner for more than a year, and to 'keep up with the Joneses' millions of people are discarding cars and appliances with many more years' life left in them.

We now talk about automation and envisage a future when we shall be able to produce goods entirely by machine controlled by a central computer. We shall see no workmen except a few who maintain the machines. But this may be a very long way off. With a suitable computer costing up to a million pounds the cost of equipping a fully automated factory would be astronomical. But in America with her vast resources and businessmen with courage and foresight this is always possible. Like Ford with his interest in the fumeless car they have their eyes always towards the future and they are ever alert for new ideas.

America is a self-supporting country with all the food, land, oil, iron ore and other raw materials she needs. This bounty of nature with her industrial efficiency has brought about a spectacular development in production over the last fifty years. Her exports of motor cars, aircraft, oil, wheat, cotton, armaments and manufactured goods of all kinds have resulted in a steady flow of the world's gold into the vaults at Fort Knox, where America stores her gold reserve in bars weighing 400 ounces. And thanks to men like Henry Ford with his revolutionary ideas she has created such vast stores of real wealth that it is impossible to imagine any decline in the foreseeable future in the value of the dollar.

Through three hundred years of trial and tribulation the Americans have brought their currency from the simple wampum to the billions of dollars now circulating, every one backed by real wealth in the form of factories, plant, power installations, railways, roads, ports—in fact, the thousand and one things that have been built and installed to help production. Three hundred years may seem a long time to stabilise their currency—probably for all time—but it is short as compared with the centuries-old struggle European countries had with their money.

Before we leave the subject of paper money it may interest you to know that two notes for £1 million have been issued in

Notes of £1,000 were the highest value ever issued in London. This 1838 design was not seen by the public; it was submitted to the Directors of the Bank of England to replace the existing note, but was not used

Britain but these were used internally by the Bank of England. At the other end of the scale, in the early eighteenth century, a note for sixpence was issued and another one for a penny. As collectors' items, they have naturally acquired a value much higher than their face value.

£1,000 notes—the largest ever issued in Britain—circulated for two hundred years until 1943, when they were discontinued. The notes were withdrawn two years later, but many have not been redeemed. Doubtless over the years some have inadvertently been destroyed, other merely retained by their owners for their value as curios.

Notes of the highest denomination ever issued for circulation in the world were those for $100,000, printed by the United States Treasury and bearing the head of President Wilson.

5 Banks
Ancient & Modern ~1

A BANK'S main business is to borrow and lend money. When you deposit money in a bank the bank, in fact, borrows it from you and then lends it out to other customers on overdraft or on loan, or it invests it in securities. The difference between the interest it allows you and the income it makes from lending or investing forms part—but not all—of the bank's profit.

Moneylending is probably as old as money itself. We know from ancient inscriptions that in Babylon, about 3000 years BC, the temples accepted deposits of money and made loans. In the Greek States of the fifth and fourth centuries BC the temples, city authorities and some private people conducted an advanced banking system. Their chief function was exchanging currencies and transferring money from one city to another, but they also had deposit accounts and lent money mainly to private persons.

In Greek literature we read about a bank in the story of Pasion and Phormion. Pasion was a slave who worked for two wealthy bankers in Athens. He was a financial genius of his time and, for his services to the state, he was given his freedom and granted full rights of citizenship. When the Greek owners retired Pasion took over control of the bank. Pasion, in turn, had a slave named Phormion, who learnt the banking business from his master, and he, like Pasion, became a free citizen. So successful was Pasion as a banker that when he retired and handed the business to Phormion, he was worth about a million pounds in modern money. At that time workmen in Athens were paid one drachma a day and Pasion's personal fortune was equal to the total yearly wages of a thousand workmen. Pasion did not accumulate his wealth by lending out money deposited by his customers. This was only a small part of his activities. He made his profits by lending his *own* money, no doubt at a very lucrative rate of interest. He was the first to adopt the dual role of public banker and *private* moneylender and this form of banking service lasted until comparatively recent times.

The Greek and later the Roman banks had to rely for their custom on private individuals. Unlike today, when governments and concerns like the nationalised industries are among the banks' biggest customers, the governments of the time had little or no connection with the banks. They relied on compulsory labour to administer the public services and they approached the banks only when they wanted to raise loans during time of war. They gave security in the form of promissory notes, which were often repaid in bad currency and sometimes repudiated if there was a change of government.

We do not know how much borrowing and lending there was in Greek and Roman times but it was probably very limited in relation to the total wealth of the people. The Greeks and Romans were not as 'money conscious' as we are today and they kept their wealth in the form of land and buildings, livestock, grain, clothing, jewels and precious metals. For this reason the development of banking remained at a standstill for many centuries until revived by the growth of trade in medieval Europe.

When the Roman Empire fell their banking system disappeared but, in the twelfth century, banking started again in some Italian cities. At this time trade and commerce were beginning to expand and traders settled their transactions in coin, sometimes for very large amounts. This was an inconvenient system and soon payments between traders were being made by transfers of money from one bank deposit account to another.

In order to do this the person making the payment had to give verbal instructions to his banker and the person receiving the money had to agree to the arrangement before witnesses. This clumsy method went on for almost two centuries until it was gradually replaced by an order on the banker written and signed by the person making the payment. This was how cheques began and, during the Middle Ages, this system of payment spread to other Italian cities, to Spain, France and as far north as Holland.

While the banks continued with their business of transferring money they could not resist the temptation to lend. They were greedy and, as they lacked expert knowledge, this got out of hand. Attracted by large profits the bankers not only lent their own money; they lent their depositors' money as well, which they often could not repay.

This reckless lending brought chaos into the banking system and this led to a public demand for banks that would transfer funds for its customers but would not indulge in moneylending. To meet this demand the first *giro* banks came into being. Like the Post Office Giro introduced in Britain some six hundred years afterwards, the banks could accept deposits and transfer funds from one account to another, but they were not allowed to make loans or grant overdrafts to their customers.

The word 'giro' is derived from the Greek word meaning ring, circle or circuit. A customer of the Post Office Giro is able to transfer funds from his account to any other *giro* account free of charge. In this way he avoids the payment of the commission usually charged by the branch banks for a similar service. The function of the giro bank is to attract funds to the system and to facilitate the movement of these funds between accounts *within the giro system*. In the early Post Office pamphlet publicising the system it was explained that the giro meant the movement of money 'round and round'. Although giro banks existed as private and public companies in Italy during medieval times the first giro system organised by the Post Office was introduced in Austria in 1883.

Up to this time all the banks were private banks, started and owned by a few wealthy people, many of whom had little or no

'T OUDE STADT HUYS.

The first Bank of Amsterdam occupied ground-floor rooms (behind the closed door on the right) in this old town hall until the building was burnt down in 1652

knowledge of banking. Provided he had sufficient capital any man could own a bank in those days whether he knew anything about the business or not. Following the failure of so many private banks people clamoured for the establishment of *public* giro banks. More people contributed capital to start these banks, which were efficiently run on professional lines. Several of these banks were founded in Italy during the fifteenth and sixteenth centuries and, in 1609, the Bank of Amsterdam was established. By this time the Dutch city had become the world's leading commercial centre.

Most of the coins that circulated at the time were clipped or forged from base metals. The Bank of Amsterdam tried to restore some order by retaining in its vaults all the bad coins that came in over the counter. In exchange the Bank credited their customers' accounts with the full face value of the coins and the customers settled their local accounts and met international bills of exchange by transfer from one account to another without the movement of coin. This new money was known as 'Bank Money' and, because of its stability, it often stood at a premium over the metallic currency. In course of time traders would accept no other money and mainly for this reason the Bank of Amsterdam practically ruled the world of commerce for the next two hundred years.

As a *giro* bank the Bank of Amsterdam was not allowed to lend money but outside pressures forced it to make loans to a few selected customers, such as city firms, public authorities and the Dutch East India Company. But, like the earlier banks, it made the mistake of lending beyond its resources and, at the beginning of the eighteenth century, it could not pay its depositors. However, the Dutch people had by this time become so used to the convenient method of making payments through the Bank that the cheques and bills continued to circulate at their face value for many years.

As a result of unwise lending the Bank's position was insecure but people continued to accept its pieces of paper as a means of payment. When anyone receives a payment the vital thing is to be sure that he can pass it on to make payments of his own.

If he can do this he can use anything—shells, pieces of metal or paper will serve the purpose. It is not the intrinsic value of the money that matters but the general *acceptability* and on this principle our modern money systems have come to depend.

In the early fourteenth century during the reign of Edward II banking was flourishing in northern Italy. The Lombards, so-called because they came from the Plains of Lombardy, decided to extend their banking business in London, and they opened their first office in what is now known as Lombard Street. Their first customers were the King, the nobles and the wealthy City merchants.

Apart from obtaining this custom the Lombards found difficulty in making headway. Most people who had money liked to keep it in their houses so that they could look at it and count it from time to time. They did not trust the banks—neither did the monarchy, apparently. When Henry VII died in 1509 a hoard of £2 million was found in his vaults. This fortune would be worth £40 million today.

In those days people did not use their money to finance trade and commerce as we do today. They hoarded it in every kind of odd place—in mattresses, secret drawers, up the chimney, in boxes with multiple locks and sewn into the upholstery of chairs and sofas. Reports of lucky 'finds' in furniture bought at auctions were frequent at one time, but they happen very rarely in these days.

Queen Elizabeth I was responsible for bringing about a change. In 1571 she opened the Royal Exchange, which was an exhibition of British goods made at the time. Many people from all over Europe came to see the display and, from then on, trade between Britain and the continent grew and has never looked back.

Until the end of the seventeenth century the only bankers in Britain were the London goldsmiths. Although there were many goldsmith bankers in Europe the people in this country were at first suspicious of the new 'bankering' trade. This was probably because the goldsmiths combined banking with their other activities—selling jewelry and gold and silver articles, exchanging foreign currency and pawnbroking. In fact, pawn-

A well known private Bank which has existed since the early seventeenth century—Child & Co, No 1 Fleet Street, London. The drawing is by Geoffrey Fletcher, the original being the property of the Bank

broking was closely associated with banking and it was many years before the two functions were separated. In course of time the goldsmiths found that the banking side of their business was outstripping their other activities and many of them became full-time bankers.

The goldsmith bankers also lent money to private borrowers and to the King. Some of them became heavily involved in lending to Charles II and were ruined when the King suspended his debts in 1672. Others survived—notably the firms of Child & Co and Hoare & Co—to become famous bankers in the eighteenth and nineteenth centuries, and they are still important London banks today.

Many of them failed because they paid too much interest to their depositors and lent their money rashly. As in earlier times in Italy the people demanded the establishment of an official bank governed by charter to carry on business on a firmer and broader basis.

In 1694 the Bank of England was founded under charter from the government. The Bank lent the government a sum of money equal to the whole of its capital, which was over a million pounds, and they charged the government 8 per cent interest on the loan, which was made partly in coin and partly in Bank of England notes. The government paid its debts with the borrowed money. These notes were the first ones issued by the new Bank but because of the prestige which the backing of the government gave it they were accepted and circulated in the business world.

In the early days the founders of the Bank did not foresee the responsibilities it has today. They intended doing the same kind of business as the goldsmiths but on a much larger scale. But from the beginning the Bank of England had a close association with the government and the prestige thus gained set it apart from other banks. Its reputation grew with developments that took place during the eighteenth and nineteenth centuries.

For a time the Bank's future was uncertain but it soon found out that the most profitable business was issuing notes and managing the government's accounts. The government borrowed

E

money from the Bank to finance the country's business until the taxes were collected and the Bank acted as agents when the government borrowed money from the public. The private side of the Bank's business declined and, although it still has some selected customers outside the government, the other banks now conduct most of this business.

Although closely connected with the government the Bank of England is in no way a state bank. It keeps the government's accounts but it also has some private customers. It is a national bank in the sense that it is confined to Britain, unlike the Bank of Amsterdam which gained a high international reputation by issuing the special 'Bank Money' mentioned earlier in the chapter.

Following the Bank Charter Act of 1844 the Bank of England had the monopoly of note issue. When the other banks stopped issuing their own notes they used Bank of England notes in their place. The banks also opened accounts with the Bank of England and settled accounts with one another by drawing cheques instead of paying in notes or coin. Thus, the Bank of England became the banker's bank. It also had custody of the country's gold reserves. By carrying out these two functions it acts as a central bank. Many countries have adopted this central bank system.

Towards the end of the eighteenth century there was a danger that the Bank would become the tool of the government. This happened when the government, at the outbreak of the war with France, borrowed money from the Bank to finance our European allies. The government had already made excessive loans to foreign states and this additional drain on the gold reserves led to the government's suspending the Bank's liability to pay gold on demand. This depletion of our reserves to meet our military expenditure and that of our allies was made worse by a further drain to bolster up a number of private banks that were crumbling. Pitt, Prime Minister at that time, remedied the situation by imposing heavy taxation and in this way he reduced the government loans. The Bank's contribution to the 'squeeze' was to restrict its private lending to private and business customers.

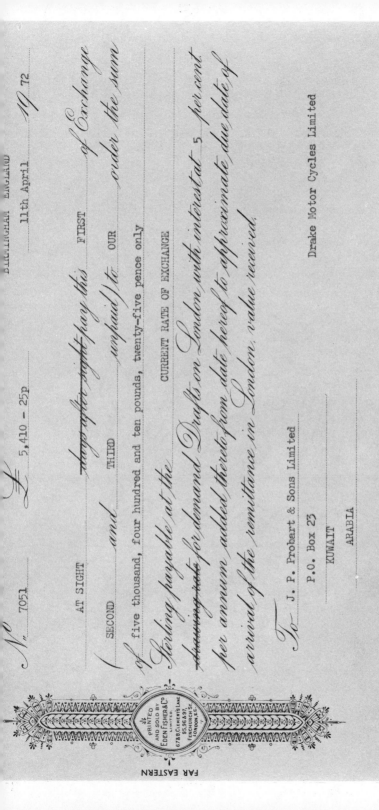

Bill of Exchange

The Bank came through these difficulties with its prestige unharmed and, during the peaceful years of the nineteenth century, this prestige increased.

Until 1826 the Bank of England had the monopoly of joint-stock banking in England. The others were small private and country banks. After 1826, the Bank opened branches in the leading business centres—Bristol, Birmingham, Liverpool, Manchester and Newcastle. At first the new branches met with opposition from the private banks because they thought that the Bank of England was poaching on their preserves, but this died down when they found that the new Bank of England was more of a help than a hindrance. Banks in each area settled their accounts through the local branch of the Bank of England and, in this way, the Bank of England became the banker's bank in the provinces as well as London.

Experience of a hundred years had taught the Bank that its first duty was to support the government in maintaining stable money conditions in the country rather than to make profit for its shareholders. In this sense and also because it had spread its tentacles to other parts of the country, it had by 1870 become a fully national institution. But because it had also become the pivot of the London money market—which is also Britain's money market—by controlling the discount rate and the country's credit policy, it had also become an international authority.

It is outside the scope of this book to deal in detail with the many complex functions of the Bank of England but it may be of interest to touch on its celebrated *Bank Rate* and its effects in this country and abroad.

Every Thursday morning at 11 am the Court of Directors of the Bank (normally about fourteen) meet to decide what interest rate to charge those who wish to 'sell' first-class bills of exchange because they want their money quickly rather than wait for the bill to mature. A bill of exchange, which is dealt with in more detail in Chapter 9, is a kind of promissory note widely used in trade and business and is the forerunner of the cheque—the difference being that a cheque is payable on demand and a bill

In the front hall of the Bank of England, Threadneedle Street, London, a Bank messenger shows the Bank Rate notice, 'No alteration in the rate of discount this day'

on some future date, generally one, two or three months ahead.

To compensate for holding the bill until it becomes due for payment the Bank make a charge. This is the Discount or Bank Rate. At the present time the decision regarding the rate is made only after consultation with the Treasury. The new or unchanged bank rate is announced at 12 o'clock mid-day.

By *custom* and not by law bank rate governs all other interest rates in the country. If the bank rate goes up all rates rise. If it is reduced the rates are lowered. With a rise in the bank rate you get more interest on your bank balance and conversely you have to pay more for your overdraft, for everything you buy on hire purchase and to the building society if you are buying your house.

You can see also how fluctuations in the bank rate affect the amount people borrow. If the rate is low people will tend to borrow more. A rise in the rate acts as a deterrent and people will borrow less. This movement in bank rate was once a more effective weapon in controlling credit than it is now in more affluent conditions, and the Bank has had to resort to other measures, such as instructing the banks to lend less money, irrespective of the interest charged, and to impose higher deposits on hire purchase transactions.

In the world's financial centres there are vast sums of money that are switched from centre to centre according to where the highest rate of interest can be earned. This has been compared to 'a flock of birds hovering about waiting to alight on the highest branch'. When the Bank of England raises the bank rate to a point where deposit rates are higher than in any other centre hundreds of millions of pounds rush into the British banks.

To do this those controlling the dollars, francs, guilders, deutschmarks and so on have to change their money into pounds sterling. This creates a demand on the foreign exchanges and the 'price' (exchange rate) of the pound rises or hardens just like any other commodity. Conversely, if the Bank lowers the rate money flows out of the country to another centre (or centres) that offers a better rate. This is the 'flight from sterling' that you may have read about in your newspapers, which brings about a drop in the exchange value of the pound.

You will see that when the exchange rate for the pound stands high we pay less in English money for our imports as we do not have to give as many pounds to acquire the foreign currency to pay for them. On the other hand, if the exchange rate is low it stimulates exports because those buying our goods do not have to put down so much of their currency to buy pounds to purchase the goods. That is why they said in November 1967 when Britain devalued the pound (ie *deliberately* reduced its value in terms of the dollar) that our exports would increase.

The choice of alternatives—whether to raise bank rate to protect the pound on the exchanges, to stimulate imports and to make borrowing dearer; or whether to lower the rate to expand credit and to give a boost to our exports—lies in the hands of the able men in the Bank of England and the Treasury who have the experience and the expertise to act in the country's best interests.

At one time criticism was levelled against the Bank for raising and lowering the Bank Rate in the interests of the banking world and so to make more profit. But in 1946 the government took over the Bank by paying out the existing shareholders and, although the mechanism of control still remains in the hands of the Bank, it now makes the decisions in consultation with the Treasury.

In September 1971 the traditional link between Bank Rate and other interest rates was severed. The joint stock banks now operate their own Base Rate, which is now $4\frac{1}{2}$ per cent, and the interest they allow on deposits and charge on loans and overdrafts is related to this Base Rate and not to Bank Rate as hitherto. This change in monetary policy has been introduced in pursuance of the Chancellor of the Exchequer's announcement in his Budget speech that the authorities wished to provide greater scope for competition between the banks, and to replace the previous credit controls by adjustments in the proportion of their deposits the banks have to lodge with the Bank of England.

6 Banks Ancient & Modern ~ 2

WE have seen how the Bank of England early in its history concentrated on issuing notes and keeping the government's accounts. It left the ordinary banking business to the London bankers, the country bankers, and later, to the large joint-stock banking companies whose branches we see in the High Street today.

The London goldsmiths originated deposit banking in this country. Their receipts were the forerunners of the bank note and their 'running cashes' came to be known as current accounts. Their main customers were the wealthy London merchants who needed large amounts of cash for their business. The goldsmiths had to persuade the merchants that it was just as safe and more convenient for them to keep their money in the goldsmiths' strong rooms as in their own office safes. When their London business grew the goldsmiths extended their services to merchants in the country and they in turn kept their bank accounts in London. In this way the London bankers' deposits kept on growing.

The merchants kept their money with the goldsmiths not only because it was safe but because they could settle accounts between one another by using cheques. The merchants conducted a large volume of mutual business and the cheque was much better for their purposes. A cheque could be made out for a specific sum of money and cancelled if lost or if a fraud was suspected. Furthermore, there was no need for the merchants to carry large sums of money in their safes or in their pockets with the risk of loss or robbery. The merchant who received a cheque did not cash it at the drawer's bank. He paid it into his own bank and the two banks adjusted the matter between them.

This is how it was done. For simplicity, let us take two Banks—Bank A and Bank B. A clerk from Bank A would call at Bank B and pick up the cheques drawn by customers of his bank and paid into Bank B. In exchange he handed to Bank B the cheques drawn by their customers and paid into his bank. The clerks added the cheques up and settled the difference in cash. This system, called the 'local clearing', is still carried out between the banks in small towns but they no longer make settlements in cash. Differences in amounts are now adjusted by means of vouchers.

The clerks who walked about London doing this work were called 'Walks Clerks'. Alarmed by the large sums of money carried about by the clerks from bank to bank the bankers rented a room where the clerks could meet and exchange their cheques. In 1770 the walks clerks met at a coffee house in Dove Court off Lombard Street. In 1805 new premises were taken and, in 1833, owing to the rapid growth of business, the Clearing House was transferred to larger premises in Lombard Street, where it has remained, except during the 1939-45 war, when it moved temporarily to the Midlands, but later returned to London.

With the exception of the Liverpool Clearing House, which deals only with cheques of £1,000 and over to serve local market needs, there are no Clearing Houses in the provinces.

The cheque soon became popular, first in London and then, in the nineteenth century, spreading rapidly to the provinces. With the growth of banks and the expansion of banking services since the turn of the present century the use of cheques has increased to such an extent that Britain now issues a total of 727 million a year and the money transferred by cheques amounts to £772,000

Bankers' Clearing House in Lombard Street, London, mid 19th century

million annually. This is about £14,000 for every man, woman and child in the country. (Banker's Clearing House Annual Report for 1970.)

In the early part of the nineteenth century the development of the use of cheques was delayed because of the heavy duty imposed on all bills of exchange with the introduction of stamp duties in 1694. Eventually the rate of duty on a cheque was standardised at one penny, and this reduction of duty was followed by a rapid expansion in their use. During the Boer War an attempt to double the duty was unsuccessful, but it was eventually raised to twopence in 1918 and remained at that level until February 1971 when cheques were freed from stamp duty with a loss to the Revenue of about £10 million a year.

When the London bankers had established the cheque system and the Clearing House in the country's mercantile centre they extended their services as agents to the rapidly growing provincial banks.

The country banker rose from the ranks of local merchants, shopkeepers, industrialists and other men of position in the locality. It was the country banker who made a vital contribution to the rapid progress of the Industrial and Agricultural Revolutions by issuing notes that were widely and readily accepted by the business community. Just as London banking grew in the seventeenth century from the goldsmith's shop the eighteenth century country banks came into being through the wealthy merchants.

James Wood became a chandler banker when he opened the Old Gloucester Bank, one of the first in the country. In 1688 Thomas Smith, a Nottingham draper, started the banking firm of Samuel Smith & Co, with branches in Nottingham and Mansfield. Thomas Smith decided to open a bank when he began to take care of the money his farmer friends received for cattle sold in the Nottingham market. With so much money in their pockets they were in danger of being robbed by the footpads who infested the countryside. In this way a drapery business became a banking business.

Sampson Lloyd, the original Lloyd of Lloyds Bank, was a

75

Birmingham ironmaster and John Taylor, who became a partner in Lloyd's first banking venture, manufactured buttons and snuff boxes.

At that time London was the only business and banking centre and all the main roads led to London. The merchants kept their own accounts with the London banks and, acting as the banks' country agents, they made the same arrangements for their new customers. Within the last thirty years a few of these agencies were still in existence in the more remote country districts.

Perhaps the most curious example of the way business was directed towards London at that time was the Welsh cattle trade. There were no railways then and the Welsh drovers herded hundreds of the Welsh black cattle along the road to London— a distance of nearly three hundred miles—to supply the London meat market. To prevent damaging their hoofs on the long, hard journey the cattle were shod like horses. Flocks of geese sometimes accompanied the cattle and they also wore specially fitted shoes made of leather.

Before starting on their journey the drovers received money from people who instructed them to settle accounts in London on their behalf. The drovers did not take the money with them. They left it at home and made the payments out of the money they received for their cattle in London.

This simple service, which probably started as a favour to friends, grew rapidly and brought into being the drover-banker and, in 1799, David Jones, a leading drover, opened a bank at Llandovery, in west Wales. It was called locally the Black Ox Bank because it issued notes bearing the picture of a black ox. In a previous chapter we have mentioned the equally quaint Bank of the Black Sheep founded in Aberystwyth about the same time.

At the beginning country banking developed slowly and by 1750 there were fewer than a dozen banks outside the London area but, within the next hundred years, these had increased to nearly five hundred. During this time two important factors had influenced their growth. First, the people had lost much of their former distrust of the banks and second, there was the advent of the mail coach.

When the first coach service from Bristol to London was opened in 1774 it marked the beginning of a crucial era in banking history. The banking centre remained in London but, with the coming of the mail coach, communications were made easier and the postal services much quicker. Until this time the country bankers did most of their banking business in the evenings, but now this side of their activities demanded more of their time and they opened their premises to banking customers throughout the day.

Taking advantage of the banking boom some tradesmen started banks with insufficient capital and little knowledge of the business. They issued notes recklessly, speculated with their customers' money and invested in risky securities. When the slump came in 1825, nearly seventy banks failed in that year. Thousands lost everything they owned because the banks did not have enough gold in their vaults to exchange for their worthless notes and had to close their doors.

The failure of so many country banks was not entirely attributable to injudicious lending and speculation. It was a period of grave financial crisis and many industrialists and others shut the doors of their factories and businesses. Moreover, the failure of the London agent frequently enough brought disaster to the country banker.

Although many of these mushroom concerns crumbled there were others, particularly those run by the Quakers, which remained as solid as rock and retained the people's confidence. One of these was Jonathan Backhouse & Company of Darlington. So great was the people's faith in this bank's reliability that they had a saying in the north, 'Safe as a Jonathan'; and everybody in the County of Durham preferred a 'Jonathan' (the name they gave to the note issued by this bank) to a Bank of England note.

As in Italy some six hundred years before, the failure of so many private concerns brought a demand for banks built on more solid foundations and conducted more efficiently. The small country banks passed away, to be replaced by a more substantial

77

*Head office of the Bank of Scotland on the Mound,
Edinburgh, in 1830*

banking structure—the joint-stock commercial bank—which
grew, like Lloyds and Barclays, from the private banks that had
weathered the storm. Other commercial banks that came into
being absorbed the remaining private banks in their stride.

We can say that we owe the beginning of our present joint-
stock commercial banking to Scotland. When the Bank of
England was formed in 1694 it was the only joint-stock bank
in existence—as opposed to the privately owned banks—and
it remained so until 1826. When the Bank of Scotland came into
being a year later it did not have this monopoly and, by 1800,
there were several commercial banks in Scotland which made
new banking history.

At that time Scotland was a relatively poor country. Why

did she lead the way in the banking field? A complete answer is difficult to find. The explanation probably lies in a combination of factors.

First, the law allowed joint-stock banks to be formed there much earlier than in England, but this is not the full explanation. Commercial banking was a new idea and new ideas can only take root and flourish in fertile ground. Here, we think, the Scottish tradition for education played its part. Another reason may have been the closely knit community life centred on the Church, which looked after not only the people's souls but also their purses. The banker in the community knew everybody—their histories, their family connections and all details about their businesses and financial affairs. This intimate knowledge of the people made lending easier and less risky. Consequently the banks flourished and grew.

Perhaps the most important reason was Scotland's poverty itself. In order to benefit from the Industrial Revolution she had to find her own capital to build new factories and to install plant and machinery. She had to induce her thrifty people to move their savings from their hiding places and take the money to the banks. Few people could resist the high rate of interest the banks offered. This resulted in a steady flow of money, which was now available to finance new industries and to expand business.

The banks allowed 4 per cent interest on their customers' deposits and charged only 5 per cent on loans and overdrafts. The difference in the rates, which is much lower than that prevailing in our banks today, not only encouraged people to put their money in the banks but also made borrowing cheaper.

Living near the Scottish border and knowing the efficiency of the Scottish banking system Thomas Joplin, a Newcastle-on-Tyne merchant, took the initiative and campaigned for years to have the Scottish system of larger banks adopted in England. In 1826 he finally triumphed and an Act was passed allowing joint-stock banks to be opened outside a radius of sixty-five miles of London. The new banks made rapid strides and, within fifteen years, there were no fewer than 115 joint-stock banks while the number of private banks had dwindled to 320.

Between the years 1833 and 1835 the London & Westminster Bank, the National Provincial Bank of England and the Birmingham & Midland Bank were established. These banks survived and grew and, with shortened names, became three of the 'Big Five'. The remaining two were Barclays Bank and Lloyds Bank.

During the next forty years there was little change in the number of banks but the balance of power was swinging to the larger joint-stock banks. They were more enterprising in opening new branches and attracting deposits. The private banks were gradually fading out of the picture because they did not have the resources to finance the needs of our rapidly expanding industries. Many of the small banks ceased to exist and over the years the growing joint-stock banks absorbed those that remained. The one exception was Barclays Bank, which was formed in 1896 by grouping together twenty small private banks into one concern.

Joint-stock banks continued to expand until recent years with branches of the leading banks in every small town. Owing to amalgamations, increased mechanisation and centralisation the present trend is to close some of the smallest branches and no doubt this pattern will continue in the foreseeable future.

So far we have dealt with the Bank of England, the country and private banks and the large commercial banks. There are others, such as the merchant banks, the savings banks, the hire-purchase banks and the Post Office Giro. All these banks offer specialised service to the public.

There are about sixty major merchant banks in this country located mainly in London. Among the most famous are Rothschilds, Schroders, Lazards and Kleinwort. The merchant bankers started as ordinary merchants dealing with foreign countries but their main business now is accepting (guaranteeing the payment of) foreign bills. You will be reading more about this in a later chapter.

Before they accept a foreign bill the merchant bankers must be certain that the trader on whose behalf they are accepting the bill can meet it when it falls due. In this way the merchant bankers became specialists in the financial reliability and integrity of foreign traders. These banks are of the highest standing and bills accepted by them, known as 'bank bills', are treated as cash and passed from hand to hand from China to Peru in the certain knowledge that they will be met when they mature. The banks charge a commission for this service.

To avoid tying up their funds too long the merchant banks discount or 'sell' the bills to the commercial banks or to special discount houses whose business it is to 'buy' the bills and hold them until they become due. As they are 'bank bills' the discount houses are sure that the bills will be paid and they will receive their money back. The discount houses do not advance the full face value of the bill. They deduct a small percentage to compensate themselves for waiting for their money. This deduction is known as the discount rate.

The four great partners in the London Money Market are the Bank of England, the deposit banks, the merchant banks and the discount houses. It is the integrity and experience of these institutions that make London the financial centre of the world.

The merchant banks also perform other functions. At one time they negotiated loans in the London Money Market on behalf of foreign governments but, when these were restricted during the Second World War, they became engaged in the issue of stocks and shares. More recently they have received deposits which they use to promote new business ventures, mergers and the like, which carry too much risk for the commercial banks. Among their other activities are bullion dealing, foreign exchange work and providing secretarial services to many charitable trusts, pension funds and similar bodies.

The first Savings Bank was opened by the Reverend Joseph Smith of Wendover in 1799. Some of his parishioners lived in distressing conditions during the winter and he suggested that, when they had a copper or two to spare, they should bring them to the church. From the pulpit he told the congregation that if they did this he would return the money at Christmas with more money as interest. The scheme worked well and so the first Penny Bank was born. Other Penny Banks followed including one at Hertford and a very famous one in the north—the Yorkshire

F

*Head office of the Yorkshire Penny Bank on East Parade,
Leeds, as altered in 1883*

Penny Bank—which grew into a substantial deposit bank issuing its own cheques.

The savings bank idea proved popular and, in 1861, the Post Office Savings Bank was started. Within fifty years there was £20 million in the bank and today the people of Britain have over £1,750 million in accounts all over the country.

Trustee Savings Banks did not arrive until the nineteenth century. They are much the same as the Post Office Savings Bank but the interest you get on your money varies with the length of time you are prepared to leave your money with the bank. You can withdraw money on demand and you can now issue cheques on a Trustee Savings Bank account.

The hire-purchase banks, such as Lombank Limited, the Mercantile Credit Co, and Bowmaker Limited, which now have branches all over the country, were set up to finance hire-purchase transactions. They charge more interest than the commercial banks because the risks they run are greater and, to attract deposits, they offer a higher rate of interest. The amount of business they can accept is governed by the funds they have available and government regulations regarding the sum of money required as a deposit. This varies from time to time according to whether the authorities decide to reduce or expand credit.

In October 1968 another Post Office venture, the National Giro, came into being. As in the fifteenth century Italian *giro* bank, money is transferred from one account to another within the system and the National Giro makes no charge for this service. But the Giro does not lend any money. The system, which is entirely automatic and mechanical, works well if every Giro customer always keeps in his account sufficient money to meet his payments but, if he is a little short owing perhaps to an oversight or miscalculation, the system breaks down and the payment is not made. In this respect there may be an advantage in maintaining your account with a commercial bank, where even in these days of the 'squeeze', a bank manager would not stop a payment if it involved a sum of only a few pence.

On 1 May 1970 the Post Office Giro developed in a new direction when it linked up with the Mercantile Credit Company to provide a personal loans scheme, thus introducing a similar service to that offered by the joint-stock banks.

Critics of the Giro say it is superfluous and a waste of public money because the commercial banks already offer to the public the same service as the Giro. Perhaps those who are responsible for its introduction have in mind Britain's probable entry into the Common Market and, as with the change to the new decimal coinage, wish to bring her in line with the continent.

7 Money and the Government

AGOVERNMENT has the sole right to issue money and this exclusive right carries with it the duty to see that there is sufficient money available to meet the needs of trade and commerce and that the value of the currency remains stable. Failure by government to adhere to these standards has often led to widespread discontent and hardship.

Having established an efficient form of money a government is faced with the problem of how to acquire money to meet its own needs. But too often a government's financial needs have been excessive. This has adversely affected the soundness of the currency, which has resulted in conflict with the people.

From the fifth century BC the Greek States had an advanced monetary system and they were followed by Egypt, Carthage and Rome. The governments relied on compulsory service by the people and payments in kind to run the country but, in time of war, they also had to raise a great deal of money to meet the increased cost.

The Greek States and other countries in the eastern Mediterranean raised funds through taxes. They imposed poll taxes, property taxes, commodity taxes, import and export duties and various tolls and dues. There was no income tax—this came centuries later. At this time the difference between capital and

Greek bronze coins of 1st to 3rd centuries AD: 1 sestertius of Ilium, obverse showing Commodus, reverse showing Hector in his quadriga; 2 sestertius of Ionia, obverse showing Antoninus Pius, reverse showing Artemis on a pedestal and two river gods

income—the money earned by capital—had not become clear enough to make income tax possible. People were taxed on their wealth, which was mainly in the form of land.

When the money collected in taxes was insufficient to meet the needs of the state the government resorted to other methods—often questionable—to raise the wind. They forced the people and the temples to give them loans. They sold public land, seized goods and ships belonging to foreigners and issued coins made of tin and bronze instead of silver. They even accepted ransom money for prisoners who had already been hanged.

The Romans had the same problems but on a larger scale.

They introduced an efficient tax-collecting system and, in times of peace, the government was able to meet its obligations and accumulate a large reserve of funds in the treasury. The treasury was called the *fiscus* from which we get our word 'fiscal'—an adjective relating to public revenue. The imperial *fiscus* not only administered the government funds, but also organised pensions for retired soldiers and lent money to assist people over difficult times.

In peace time the value of money in ancient Rome was steady but, when the Empire was challenged from outside, wars became inevitable. With the increased cost to the state the financial position deteriorated. To remedy the situation the state increased taxes and this led to tax evasion. This evasion increased the burden on those who were forced to pay and it made it more difficult for the government to meet its commitments. We believe that this weakening of the country's finances was one of the important causes that led to the fall of the Roman Empire.

For many centuries after the break-up of the Roman Empire money seemed to go out of fashion. Banking almost disappeared, to be brought to life again in Italy in the twelfth century. Money became less important to governments and to commerce. Governments conducted the affairs of the nation by relying on services given by the people rather than on money.

As in Germany, all freemen in England in Anglo-Saxon times were obliged to do military service but only the more intelligent type of peasant took part. As they were more progressive in the arts of war than the rulers, the military power in Europe passed into the hands of the knight of the castle supported by his picked and trained followers. The superiority of William the Conqueror's knights in armour over Harold's peasants decided the Battle of Hastings and for the next three centuries the feudal knight and his retainers held sway.

As the methods of conducting wars became more advanced the cost increased. Bows and arrows ended the superiority of the knight in armour at the battles of Crecy and Poitiers and the bowmen, in turn, were displaced by the invention of firearms and the Swiss Mercenaries—trained soldiers who hired themselves out to any country that could pay for their services. The rising cost of war and growing commerce brought about increasing demands for money from both governments and the people.

In the twelfth century intense rivalry between the Italian cities brought on many costly wars. The city authorities met this cost by forcing people to lend them money at a low rate of interest. In acknowledgement of the money they lent the people received bonds. Unlike money borrowed in previous times to meet the cost of war these were long-term loans and, like government securities today, the bonds were bought and sold on the open market. Because the interest was low the market price of the bonds was low, and those people compelled by circumstances to turn their bonds back into cash often lost considerable sums of money.

This hardship brought about the need for some method of borrowing from the people that was not compulsory and brought a better return. An entirely voluntary system in the form of annuities was introduced. In return for the loan the people received a yearly payment during their lives and sometimes after they died to provide for their dependants. In Italy, France, Holland and Germany city authorities raised money in this way until the fifteenth century.

In Britain conditions were different from those in Europe. It was mainly a country of landlords and peasants. Trade and commerce were just beginning and there was no wealthy merchant class from whom the Crown could borrow money compulsorily or otherwise. In the Middle Ages the sale of wool to Italy and Flanders was by far the most important item in the British export trade and the Crown received substantial sums of money from the export duties. We shall see in a later chapter how the financial side of this trade was controlled by the Italian bankers, who combined this activity with their method of sending Papal dues to Rome.

Until the end of the thirteenth century the Crown borrowed money from the Jews. In law the Jews were regarded as the King's personal chattels and they were powerless to resist his demands. But from the fourteenth century onwards the Crown relied more and more on revenue from the export of wool. At this time England was at war with France and Scotland and the King needed more money. By a private arrangement with the wool merchants and without the authority of Parliament, Edward I imposed a tax of forty shillings on each sack of wool they exported. In return he granted the merchants certain trading privileges and this favouritism brought on trouble between the people and the merchants.

In spite of unceasing conflict with Parliament and the people Edward I and his successors continued to make private arrangements with the merchants and, by the middle of the fourteenth century, during the Hundred Years' War, the King was in serious financial trouble. Although Parliament had granted him large sums of money from taxes they were not enough for the King and he imposed further wool taxes. He also seized large quantities of wool from the merchants, which he pledged as security for his loans, raising money against the taxes the wool would bring in. He first borrowed from the Italian merchant bankers but, because he was bad at repaying his loans, several of the merchants became bankrupt. He then borrowed from syndicates of merchants to whom he gave the wool monopoly, but they suffered the same fate.

Another way the kings raised money was by reducing the weight of the coins. By the end of the fifteenth century the silver coins weighed less than half what they had been two hundred years earlier. By 1560, when Queen Elizabeth I minted new coins of standard weight and fineness, the coins in circulation had but a fraction of the silver they had contained when they were first made.

During the reign of Henry VII the Crown's finances were more stable. He was a careful, economical man who accumulated a vast amount of wealth, which he lent to his people. On the other hand his son, Henry VIII, was as extravagant as his father had been cautious. He spent large sums of money on himself and his Court but he also has the credit for increasing the number of ships in our Navy from seven to fifty-three. He was involved in costly wars with France and Scotland and, towards

Among Henry VIII's vast expenses one of the most praiseworthy was for increasing the navy from seven to fifty-three ships. This 16th century painting of 'The Embarkation of Henry VIII at Dover, 1520', by an unknown artist, is in the Royal Collection at Hampton Court

the end of his reign, he also had to deal with rebellions in England and Ireland. Owing to the influx of gold and silver from America which brought about an increase in the amount of money in circulation, this was a time of rapidly rising prices and this trend continued until the seventeenth century.

Henry VIII tried in every possible way to raise funds but there was insufficient money available in Britain to meet his demands. He then borrowed from moneylenders on the continent. His successors continued to borrow money from abroad but their supplies were cut off when Antwerp lost its importance as a financial centre. Henry VIII also reduced the weight of the coins. Previous kings had done this to make a modest profit, but he reduced the metal to such an extent that the gold or silver in the coins was only one-sixth of what it had been when he came to the throne.

For the next hundred years or so prices rose steeply. The cost of war and amount of the King's personal expenditure also increased. This was far greater than the King's income and Parliament was reluctant to introduce additional taxes to bridge the gap. This led to the bankruptcy of the Crown. As an example, Charles II had not enough money and could not get credit to buy munitions and stores for his Navy so that it could sail to meet the Dutch fleet, which had penetrated up the Medway.

The Crown tried to increase its income by all kinds of dubious means. It imposed unfair taxes, like 'ship money' on inland towns. It gave monopolies to merchants in exchange for loans and sold off Crown lands, including those that were freed with the break-up of the monasteries. This action by the Crown was an important factor in the quarrels that led up to the Civil War.

In those days the King's Exchequer did not issue receipts for loans. Instead it used tallies. A tally was a hazel stick in which notches were cut to represent the amount of money received. The stick was split down the middle—the Exchequer keeping one part and the other part being handed to the person making the loan. This was the only evidence that a loan had been made to the Crown and holders of the tallies had difficulty in redeeming them and getting their money back.

91

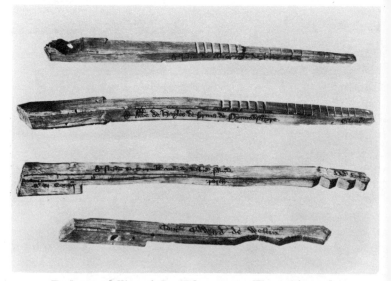

Exchequer tallies of the 13th century. The writings show the names of persons who had paid money into the Exchequer and the nature of the account, and the notches represent the sums paid

In 1693 Parliament passed an Act providing that every tally should be accompanied by an official acknowledgement of the loan called an 'order of loan'. These were the first Exchequer Orders, to be followed later by Exchequer Bills. Later the orders were issued for round sums and passed from hand to hand like bank notes. These orders might have been our first paper currency but this was knocked on the head in 1672, when Charles II refused to repay over £1 million of these loans.

The Revolution of 1689 and the war with France placed a great strain on the King's purse and his debts rose to £20 million by 1697. About this time several important things happened that revolutionised the money system. Parliament took control of the country's finances; the Bank of England was formed; the government now borrowed for short terms with Exchequer Bills instead of tallies and it marked the beginning of the National Debt as opposed to the King's private debt.

When the Bank of England was founded in 1694 the government immediately borrowed over £1 million to pay its debts.

Within a year or two it was borrowing again by issuing Exchequer Bills. These receipts issued by the Exchequer for short-
term loans were rather like bank notes. They passed from hand
to hand like bank notes but had to be endorsed each time. The
government borrowed as little as £5 from many lenders but later
withdrew bills for small amounts. Exchequer Bills for more
substantial sums remained for many years the principal method
by which the government borrowed money for short terms.

The English internal National Debt began in 1693 when the
government raised £1 million by means of annuities of various
kinds. This was followed by the £1 million borrowed from the
Bank of England in 1694 and large loans from the chartered
companies like the East India Company and the South Sea
Company. This borrowing from the companies came to an end
with the bursting of the South Sea Bubble in 1720.

Confidence in the government was growing, and the next
step was to borrow money from a wider range of people. The
8 per cent interest on the Bank of England loan was proving a
burden and, in the 1730s, the government issued long-term
loans to the general public at 3 per cent interest. From then
until the defeat of Napoleon in 1815 the government borrowed
nearly £700 million from the people by issuing further stocks.

These new government loans were very different from the
doubtful loans raised by needy kings in the past. Parliament
had now gained control of the country's income and expenditure
and the National Debt was secured by the whole of the country's
revenue. The government paid the interest regularly and loans
were promptly repaid when they became due. People looked on
government stocks as the safest investment next to the ownership
of land.

At that time the government's administration of the country
was only just beginning and it would then have been impossible
to mobilise an army by conscription, to confiscate anything that
the government required and to impose controls on the people
like those experienced by the British in two world wars. Governments had to buy the sinews of war with hard cash and its ability
to wage war was limited by the amount of money it could raise.

The government now had the power to borrow vast sums of money by issuing long-term stocks and it could cover its short-term needs with Exchequer Bills. The Bank of England became the government's agent by managing the issue of Exchequer Bills and supervising the National Debt. As a result the reputation the Bank gained assured its outstanding position over all the other banks.

For most of the time between 1756 and 1815 England was involved in major wars. The National Debt rose from £71 million in 1748 to £820 million at the end of the Napoleonic War. The greatest cost was incurred in the struggle with France in the early nineteenth century. The government not only had to send large sums of money to meet military costs but also had to make loans to its allies. Prices rose in Britain and people were losing faith in the bank note. In 1797, rumours of a French invasion caused them to demand gold at the Bank for their notes and this led to the suspension of payment in coin, which lasted until 1821.

In relation to the country's wealth when the Napoleonic War ended the National Debt must have been almost as large as it is today. In the nineteenth century, however, wars were few and the long period of peace enabled the government to repay some of the Debt. By 1914 it had been reduced to £650 million. But by the end of the First World War the debt had increased almost ten-fold to £6,000 million and by 1945-6 it had reached over £25,000 million.

When peace returned after the 1939-45 war the government nationalised the Bank of England, the coal, gas and electricity industries, the railways, part of the steel industry, and road and rail transport. It paid out the shareholders in the industries taken over by giving them government securities in exchange for their shares. It also lent money to develop the nationalised industries, and to public corporations and to local authorities to build new houses, schools and hospitals. In most of the post-war years the government had a Budget surplus but this was not nearly large enough to cover its investments.

In the past governments borrowed to meet the needs of war

and any government who borrowed in peace time was looked upon as being incompetent. Now things had changed. The government became a regular peacetime borrower and as a result the National Debt has risen to the figure of £33,000 million.

It is estimated that about one half of the total personal wealth of people in Britain is made up of government stocks and bonds. This is a measure of their faith in the government's integrity and stability and of their confidence in the future. In spite of two world wars and the slump of the 1930s this trust has not wavered. When stock falls due for repayment the government gets the money from the issue of further stocks and there has never been a shortage of subscribers. The government pays the interest on these stocks and bonds from the National Loans Fund and, in the financial year ending March 1970, this amounted to £1,458 millions. Money is passed into the National Loans Fund by transferring the annual Budget surplus, ie the difference between what the government receives in revenue and what it spends. In the same year this was £2,444 million.

The Budget is the plan or blueprint of the government's financial operations and covers a period of twelve months— from the beginning of April of one year to the end of the following March. The purpose of the Budget is not only to raise revenue and to meet expenditure. It is the way the government manages the country's economic life. In his annual speech the Chancellor of the Exchequer not only puts forward his proposals for raising money by taxation but also reviews the government's finances and the state of the nation. His new measures are later set out in a Finance Bill which does not become law until the end of the following July. But most of the tax changes proposed in the Budget come into effect immediately.

Treasury officials and others begin work on the Budget soon after the previous one is presented. By November the Board of Inland Revenue, the Customs and Excise and other departments who collect revenue have to submit estimates of the money they will receive in the current year, and what they expect to receive in the following year if the tax rates remain the same. Between November and January other government

Mr Anthony Barber, Chancellor of the Exchequer, with his despatch box on Budget Day 1972

departments prepare estimates of what they are likely to spend in the coming year. Their figures have to be agreed by the Treasury and submitted to Parliament.

The Chancellor works on his Budget throughout the year. He keeps an eye on economic trends and consults officials in the Treasury and the Revenue Departments. Other departments are also brought into the picture but only in so far as they may be involved in special matters dealt with in the Budget. Great secrecy has to be observed so that there will be no opportunity for persons to turn Budget information to their own financial advantage. The general rule is that a person is not consulted unless work on the Budget cannot go on without him. Even then he sees only those parts of the Budget that concern him. The rest is kept secret from him.

The original purpose of the Budget was to enable the government to raise sufficient funds to meet expenses in the same financial year. But now that the government is the country's biggest spender and takes much more in taxes, both these factors have an important influence on the level of output and the distribution of our resources. Today those who prepare the Budget are concerned with the balance between the goods and services that are produced and the total demand made on them.

Taxation provides the government with an important means of influencing this demand. For instance, an increase in direct taxation (like income tax) or indirect taxation (like purchase tax) on consumers will reduce the amount they spend on goods and services and will therefore reduce demand. By adjusting taxation the government can also provide incentives for manufacturers and other producers, to increase exports and to encourage savings.

Before the Budget the government forecasts the growth in the value of goods and services we can provide and the demand for these resources. If the forecasts show that this potential growth will be in balance with demand an adjustment in taxes may not be necessary. But if we are not buying the goods and services we produce, the government can take action through the Budget to stimulate demand by reducing taxes so that we can have more money to spend. On the other hand, if demand is greater than expected, the government can slow it down by increasing taxes.

The table overleaf, *in millions of pounds*, shows the sources of the government's income and how it spent the money in the financial year ended March, 1970.

The Budget Surplus—the difference between the money collected (£15,266 million) and the money spent (£12,822 million), which is £2,444 million—is transferred to the National Loans Fund, from which the government meets the interest on its stocks and bonds.

INCOME £
(millions)

INLAND REVENUE

Income Tax	4,900
Corporation Tax (Tax on companies)	1,687
Death Duties	365
Surtax	255
Other Taxes and Duties	269
	7,476

CUSTOMS AND EXCISE

Tobacco	1,143
Purchase Tax	1,110
Oil	1,302
Spirits, Beer and Wine	862
Betting and Gaming	119
Others	416
	4,952

Motor Vehicle Duties	417
Selective Employment Tax	1,888
Broadcast Receiving Licences	101
Other Receipts	432
Total	15,266

EXPENDITURE £
(millions)

CIVIL SUPPLY

Government and Finance	198
Commonwealth and Foreign	305
Home and Justice	265
Communications, Trade and Industry	2,816
Agriculture	386
Local Government, Housing and Social Services	5,043
Education and Science	451
Public Buildings and Common Governmental Services	281
Others	67
	9,812

DEFENCE BUDGET

Defence	1,830
Ministry of Technology	200
Ministry of Public Buildings and Works	174
	2,204

Payment to National Loans Fund	513
Other Services	293
Total	12,822

(*Source: Financial Statement and Budget Report* 1970-1)

In addition to the internal debt of £33,000 million the government borrows for short or medium terms large amounts of money in American dollars from the International Monetary Fund or from foreign banks in connection with its foreign exchange transactions. In recent years these loans have ranged from £889 million in June 1967 to £3,363 million in December 1968. In December 1969 the figure was £2,664 million.

The composition of the National Debt as at 31 March 1969—the last date to which details are available at the time of writing—is given below with an outline explanation of the less-familiar items:

		£ millions
Marketable Securities		
Dated	15,690	
Undated	3,539	
		19,229
Annuities		478
Debt to Bank of England		11
National Savings Certificates		2,016
Defence Bonds		185
National Development Bonds		578
Premium Savings Bonds		715
National Savings Stamps and Gift Tokens		36
Tax Reserve Certificates		344
Floating Debt		
Treasury Bills	5,741	
Ways and Means Advances	338	
		6,079
TOTAL INTERNAL DEBT		29,671
External Debt		
Payable in Sterling	2,060	
Payable in Other Currencies	2,253	
		4,313
TOTAL NATIONAL DEBT		33,984

MONEY AND THE GOVERNMENT

We have seen that some government finance is raised by borrowing and the total of the money borrowed at any one time is called the National Debt. In peacetime the volume of the Debt does not vary greatly from year to year and Chancellors of the Exchequer resist the temptation to burden people by excessive borrowing to meet current needs, but in wartime things are very different.

In 1914 the Debt stood at £650 million but, by the end of the First World War, it had increased by more than ten times. In 1939 it was about £7,000 million but reached £25,000 by 1946. In the twenty-five years between 1946 and 1971 it increased by only £8,000 million, reaching the present figure of £33,000 million.

This total appears frightening but, to bring it in perspective, we have to remember that the purchasing power of the £ has fallen greatly over the years and that the Debt, as gigantic as it is, represents only a little over twice the income from the Budget.

The main item in the External Debt payable in sterling is £1,860 million borrowed from the International Monetary Fund and the International Development Association, and about 97 per cent of the Debt payable in other currencies is represented by loans from the United States and Canadian Governments.

(*Source: Whittaker's Almanack* 1971)

Marketable Securities are government stocks that are quoted on the Stock Exchange. Carrying a government guarantee these bonds are classed as gilt-edged and these stocks, with those of the nationalised industries, comprise the section *British Funds* which appears at the head of the Stock Exchange quotations in your daily newspaper.

Most of the stocks are dated, that is, they carry a guarantee both of income and date of redemption. The stocks are grouped in three sections—those with fewer than five years to run ('shorts'), those with five to fifteen years to run ('mediums') and those with over fifteen years to maturity. The longest of these is the $5\frac{1}{2}\%$ Treasury Stock which is redeemed between the years 2008 and 2012.

Undated stocks, of which $3\frac{1}{2}\%$ War Loan is the largest issue, carry a guaranteed income but no promise of redemption at any time. Generally speaking the market prices of British Funds vary according to the redemption dates. The highest-priced are the short-dated stocks and the lowest the long-dated ones. Because they carry no government guarantee of redemption the prices of the undated stocks are substantially lower than the prices of the dated stocks. The market price of the undated stocks varies mainly in accordance with ruling interest rates.

Although the market price may be low an undated stock, like $3\frac{1}{2}\%$ War Loan, is an excellent investment from the point of view of income. If the current price is, say, £40, for an investment of £100 you can acquire £250 of stock and, at a return of $3\frac{1}{2}\%$ for every £100 stock, you receive an annual yield of £8·75 on your investment.

If ruling interest rates are high and offer a better alternative investment holders will sell their War Stock and invest the proceeds elsewhere. On the other hand if interest rates are low people will invest in War Stock for the better yield. There will be an increased demand for the stock and the price will rise.

Annuities are sums of money advanced to the Exchequer which are repayable by equal amounts annually over a number of years, or—in the case of life annuities—until the death of the holder. The rate of interest allowed on the annuities is low and most of them terminate in the years 1976-80.

Tax Reserve Certificates are sold by the government to tax-payers as a short-term investment whereby they can set aside, up to two years in advance, money they will pay in direct taxes when they become due. Tax-free interest is allowed from the date of purchase until the tax is due. The certificates are not transferable and can be redeemed at par without interest.

Floating Debt. This is the total of the government's borrowing for periods not exceeding three months and is mainly represented by Treasury Bills. The government spends money in advance of its revenue and the spending tends to flow evenly throughout the year. Revenue comes in in concentrated periods and, to bridge the gap, the need for short-term borrowing arose. This temporary borrowing is now so large that it has become a permanent item, but is nevertheless made up of short-term loans.

The much smaller section of the Floating Debt—Ways and Means Advances—are the total temporary loans made to the Exchequer on a day to day basis mainly by the Bank of England. This borrowing becomes necessary when the Exchequer's cash requirements have been underestimated and the money is lent overnight to make up any deficit.

External Debt. This is probably the most important section of the National Debt. Unlike debts owing to people and institutions within the British economy this represents a real burden on the resources. Whether the debts are payable in sterling or in foreign currency the result is an export of goods and services which could be available for consumption at home or to purchase imports.

Subject to policy decisions by the Treasury the control and management of the National Debt is in the hands of the Bank of England and, at the present time, this is the Bank's main function. The management of the Debt calls for a high degree of efficiency so as to reduce to a minimum any dislocation in the national finances. For example, the Bank must see that the maturity dates of the marketable securities are so arranged that too many do not fall together within a short period, thus imposing a burden within this period to repay the investments or to float fresh loans for this purpose.

An important factor is the effect of the National Debt on interest rates. To pay interest on a debt of £33,000 million out of current taxation is a considerable item and it would be to the Exchequer's advantage if interest rates were kept low, but it is sometimes necessary—as in recent times—to raise interest rates to dampen down inflation in the interests of the economy as a whole.

Before considering where the burden of the National Debt lies it is well to appreciate the difference between the public debt and the debts of private persons. A private debt is an asset for one person, who holds a claim for repayment, and a liability for another. When the net assets of all private persons and institutions in the country are aggregated the two cancel out and the value of the real assets remain.

National Debt transactions mean transfers of debt between

one person and another. Interest is paid out of taxation and a loan is repaid by raising fresh money. An internal national debt (ie the debt owed to the citizens of a country) is therefore not a burden, as is sometimes thought. Transfers of debts between people in a community make some richer and some poorer, but the *real* wealth of the country is not reduced and an internal debt cannot threaten a country with national bankruptcy.

The existence of a national debt, however, cannot add to the real wealth of a community as a whole but holders of government securities count these investments as part of their *personal* wealth. When we calculate the net assets of the private sector of a community we have to exclude all private debts, but we must take into account the private holding of a public debt.

Another important difference between private and public debt is that the former is normally backed by real wealth. This is true in a degree of public debt (eg the assets of nationalised industries) but a large part of the public debt has been incurred not to create wealth but to meet the cost of war. The assets thus acquired have gone up in smoke.

The security of the National Debt is not the real wealth that may or may not support it but the power of the government to raise money from the community. To the extent that public debt held by private citizens is not backed by real wealth, the total of public and private assets therefore exceeds the real wealth of the community.

Can a country's national debt be allowed to increase indefinitely and how will the growth of the debt affect future generations?

In *A Study in Public Finance*, 3rd edition, the eminent authority A. C. Pigou states: 'It is true that loans *raised from foreigners* (the External Debt) entail a burden represented in interest and sinking fund on future generations in the borrowing country. But interest and sinking fund on *internal loans* are merely transfers from one set of people in the country to another set, so that the two sets together—future generations as a whole— are not burdened at all.'

The question is a complex one and, despite this authoritative pronouncement, the old controversy about whether government

103

borrowing imposes a burden on the future is from time to time given a new airing. Some economists hold the view that growth in the national debt will have some effects on generations to come and give the following reasons in support of their opinion.

As the debt grows so does the total interest payable to the holders of the debt. This means an increasing transfer of income from the general taxpayers to the smaller group of debt holders. This will tend to emphasise any existing inequalities in the distribution of income.

The growth in public debt might absorb capital that would be available to the private sector of the community. Future generations would inherit less capital wealth and the goods and services produced by this wealth would be reduced. Against this we must consider that peacetime expansion of a national debt, eg the nationalisation of industry, would increase the assets of the public sector and future generations would consequently benefit from the flow of goods and services these would provide.

With a rapidly growing national debt a government might be tempted to adjust the levels of taxation in its own interests as a borrower, ie to attract investment or to pay interest, and not to use taxation as an economic instrument to control the level of demand for goods and services when necessary.

These authorities also say that the expansion of the public debt may also affect the present generation. The introduction of a monetary policy designed to assist government borrowing might impose restrictions that would be disadvantageous to the economy as a whole. Consequently a reduction in the rate of growth of the debt or a freezing for an appropriate period could bring about a more efficient monetary policy. If a government did not find it necessary to issue fresh bonds and was able to re-finance existing ones from alternative resources a more flexible policy in long-term rates could follow.

Opposing these arguments there is the overriding factor that a good government is concerned with long-term growth of the economy and is not likely to discourage investment by the private sector. Management of the national debt is accordingly arranged with this end in view.

8 Foreign Exchanges

WHEN people living in different countries trade with one another this usually involves an exchange of currencies. If British people buy goods in Paris they pay for them in French francs which they get by changing their travellers' cheques at any of the many banks who give this service. Each of these banks is a small foreign exchange market, but the markets that deal with the financing of foreign trade are large highly organised departments of the leading banks in every country. We shall be dealing with the interesting and complicated work carried out by these markets later in the chapter.

Until quite modern times travelling merchants conducted a large part of international trade. They carried their goods abroad and sold them for local currency. They used the currency to buy local goods which they brought home with them. When import and export trade works in this way there is no need for the exchange of currencies. Neither is it necessary when the exporter and importer agree to settle their accounts in the same currency. British currency is an example, and nearly one-third of the world's trade is financed by payments in sterling.

We can trace the exchange of currency to the remote past. Money-changing in the ancient world was a complicated business. Many cities and states issued their own coins and they were

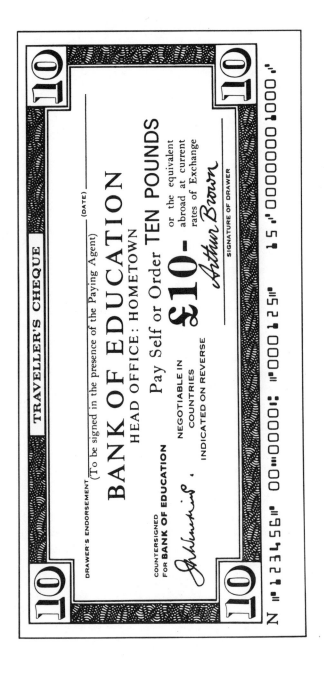

Traveller's cheque, which the traveller can buy from his own bank before his journey and which he can exchange for foreign currency at a foreign bank

made from different metals—gold, silver, electrum (an alloy of gold and silver), copper and bronze. To add to the difficulties many of the coins were worn, clipped, mutilated and counterfeit. The money changers became expert in dealing with this disorderly mass of coins and their business was profitable.

In Greece during the fifth and fourth centuries BC the bankers' main job was exchanging coins. We know from the Bible that Jesus drove out the money-changers from the temple in Jerusalem. For several centuries before this many of the temples in the Middle East changed coins as well as pursuing other banking activities. Exchanging coins remained an important business for hundreds of years but as time went on trade in coins diminished, to be replaced by bills of exchange.

The transport cost of large shipments of gold over long distances on land and over the sea with the risk of robbery was the incentive to find some other way of making payments between country and country. From Greek literature we learn that bankers, several hundred years before the Birth of Christ, devised a simple method of doing this.

If A, a merchant in Athens, wanted to pay a large amount of gold to C, another merchant overseas, he handed the gold to B, another Athenian merchant. B would instruct merchant D in the foreign country, who owed him money, to hand the equivalent amount of gold to A on his arrival. On his journey to the foreign country A carried a letter written by B to D giving him instructions to hand over the gold. As none of these letter instructions exists we do not know whether this document was a bill of exchange in modern terms. Nevertheless, this letter was the means of transferring a large amount of gold from one country to another without any exporting of metal or coin.

Records show that bankers in Genoa in the twelfth century had a method of transferring money between countries by written instructions only. By the thirteenth century there was an organised system of international payments between the main commercial centres of Europe. Merchants in Italy and Spain settled accounts between themselves and with merchants in other countries by asking their bankers to give written instructions to

107

their agents, who were also bankers in the various countries, to make payments on their behalf.

Most of the trade in Europe at that time was carried out by travelling merchants who moved from place to place but who got together at certain times at the great international fairs. These fairs were held in Champagne and Lyon in France, Flanders in Belgium, and Spain.

The traders bought and sold goods in large quantities at the fairs but they used little cash. Instead, a banker kept a record of all transactions and, at the end of the fair, he would strike a balance in his books between one merchant and another. If this balance was small the merchants settled in spot cash but they cleared large accounts by means of a bill of exchange. The merchant to whom the money was owed (the creditor) drew a bill on the merchant who owed the money (the debtor) which would be payable at the next fair. In this way the debtor undertook to settle the account on a future date and, while the creditor held the bill, he had a claim on the debtor.

A bill of exchange drawn in the currency of a particular country is a 'claim' on money in that country. For example, if a British exporter draws a bill on an American buyer for goods he has shipped the exporter will have so many dollars available to him in America when the buyer meets the bill. The exporter can use the dollars either to buy goods in America or to pay off any debts he may have in that country. If he does not want to use the dollars for these purposes he can have them converted into sterling. But there may be other British traders whose need for dollars is more urgent than his and if the 'price', ie the rate of exchange, is right he will 'sell' the bill to them in exchange for their pounds. In this way he transfers to them his 'claim' on the dollars.

The transfer of Papal dues to Rome in the thirteenth century is a good early example of how large sums of money passed from one country to another without the movement of any metal or coin. The Pope's Representative in England, for instance, collected the dues, which he paid to the Italian merchant bankers in London. At that time the English had a growing export in wool and the exporters obtained payment from buyers in Italy by drawing bills on them in lire. The merchant bankers used the money they held from the Papal dues to buy these bills from the exporters. The exporters received settlement in sterling and, when the bills fell due for payment, the bankers paid over the Italian lire to the Vatican.

The international payment system of the thirteenth and fourteenth centuries became a sort of clearing house for debts. Traders paid their debts abroad by buying claims on currency in their creditors' country. A credit in one country could by sale and purchase be used to pay off a debt in any other country. Accounts were kept between each financial centre and were settled at regular intervals.

By the end of the fourteenth century the bill of exchange and the way it was used in international payments reached a form that changed little during the next five hundred years. The European fairs declined and transactions came under the control of bankers and their banker-agents in different countries. When trade moved northwards Italy lost its position as a leading financial centre to Bruges, followed by Antwerp and finally by Amsterdam. As the volume of business increased and markets became much more organised other centres sprang up all over Europe.

Amsterdam was by far the most important foreign exchange centre during the seventeenth and eighteenth centuries but, from the sixteenth century, London had also become an important foreign currency market. In 1571 Queen Elizabeth I opened the Royal Exchange and this was the main centre for foreign exchange business until the nineteenth century.

By this time nearly all the world's trade and other international transactions were financed by the bill of exchange and the volume of business connected with the purchase and sale of 'claims' to foreign currency increased accordingly. The foreign exchange markets, first run by simple money-changers, were gradually organised by dealers in claims on a massive scale. But with the telephone and now telex the speed of transactions between centres has increased a thousand times as compared with

Queen Elizabeth I at the Royal Exchange, London, in 1571

the letters and messages of medieval times, which took weeks to reach their destination.

The London foreign exchange market acts as a clearing house through which purchases and sales of foreign currencies are made. Its business comes from transactions between the banks and their customers, between banks and banks, and between English banks and foreign banks.

While dealings between different foreign exchanges are organised in the same way, the business of local markets is based on two different systems. In Britain, the United States, Canada, Switzerland and some other countries the foreign exchange market is not any special place or location like, say, the Stock Exchange. The term 'market' is a collective word meaning a number of buyers and sellers in continuous contact with each other for the purpose of transacting business. They conduct their business through a network of private telephone links with the foreign exchange brokers and by telephone or telex with foreign banks abroad.

On the continent the foreign exchange markets are actual locations where dealers meet every business day. Such markets existed in almost every country from medieval times until the early part of this century. In France, West Germany, Italy and the Netherlands they have survived until the present day. Usually the market is situated in the *Bourse* or Stock Exchange and, although it has nothing to do with transactions in stocks and shares, it works in much the same way. Dealers buy and sell foreign exchanges like any other commodity and the 'price' —the rate of exchange—is influenced by the supply and demand for the commodity.

Until the end of the First World War officials of the merchant banks met twice weekly at the Royal Exchange to conduct foreign exchange business. But, even by that time, the bulk of this business was in the hands of the commercial banks and the foreign exchange brokers so, when the old market closed, it made little difference.

The London foreign exchange market is run by dealers and brokers. The dealers are selected from men who have had

111

A modern For-eign Exchange Dealing Room at a bank

experience in the foreign branches of the banks. They work in a department of the bank called the Dealing Room, and in a large bank up to a hundred dealers can be seen, each sitting at a desk facing a switchboard on which there is a complex of red and green lights. From his switchboard the dealer is connected by direct telephone to a number of brokers and on outside lines he communicates with his customers and banks overseas.

The broker specialises in certain currencies or a group of currencies. He is an expert in his particular field. He concentrates on the movements of the currency in the world markets and knows— or can find out in seconds—who has a particular currency to sell and who wants to buy. If a bank customer wants to buy Danish currency to meet a payment in Copenhagen his telephone call is passed to a dealer. The dealer contacts by telephone one or more brokers who specialise in Scandinavian currencies. There may be several brokers who can supply the currency. The dealer then searches round for the best bargain, ie rate of exchange, for his customer. When a broker secures the business he earns a fee called brokerage.

Foreign exchange transactions can either be 'spot' or 'forward'. A 'spot' transaction is one which takes place immediately a rate of exchange is agreed between the dealer and broker. In a 'forward' transaction the rate is agreed *now* but the exchange of currencies will not take place until some future date. On this future date the rate of exchange may have fluctuated violently in favour of either the buyer or the seller but the rate that applies to this particular transaction is the 'forward' rate agreed earlier.

Let us suppose that a British importer is negotiating the purchase of a shipment of iron ore from Sweden for delivery in, say, three months' time, when payment would be due. Rather than take the risk that the rate of exchange will move against him in the meantime he asks his bank to quote a rate at which he can buy an amount of money in Swedish kronor on a date three months ahead. The bank dealer, with the aid of his broker or brokers, will now search the markets for some arrangement that will meet his customer's requirements. Having agreed the price of the ore with the Swedish exporter the importer can now calculate

H

exactly what he has to pay in sterling for the shipment and thereby incurs no loss if the rate of exchange on the actual date of payment is not in his favour.

The foreign exchange dealer must be widely experienced in the operation of the foreign exchanges. He must be cool-headed, quick-witted and reliable. Such a man must be able to take the responsibility for involving his bank in contracts amounting to millions of pounds on the telephone alone. Every deal is completed by word of mouth before any written contract is drawn up.

Business is transacted at amazing speeds and the dealer has to make up his mind in a split second and take quick decisions. He must be well informed in the way the markets are moving and must react quickly to any changes. Often he has no time to refer important matters to his superiors and he has to act on his own judgment. Mistakes are made easily and they are costly.

You can get no better picture of the hectic life of a foreign exchange dealer than the following extract from an article written by Jack R. Higgins, himself an experienced dealer, which has been taken from the booklet *A Day in the Life of a Banker*, issued by the Institute of Bankers.

> *Bearing in mind that his spoken word is committing his bank, no words are ever spoken lightly, whatever the tone or the chatter that may be involved. Contracts involving literally millions of pounds are passed through these telephones with never a word on paper until after the completion of a deal.*
>
> *Whilst the customers of the bank meet and are influenced by management, heads of departments, cashiers and the representatives of the bank, to the banker overseas the foreign exchange dealer is often his principal contact, and impressions made by foreign exchange dealings bear lusty fruit.*
>
> *By now the whole bank of his switchboard is coloured with red lights, turning to green as he and his assistants connect up to the calls. Calls from customers, calls from foreign banks overseas, calls from the brokers. Some merely seeking information, some seeking rates on which to base their day's work. There will be calls from Paris, Amsterdam, Copenhagen, Brussels, Hamburg and many other financial centres. Some*

with genuine propositions, some hoping for an advantageous quotation somewhere in the list. Many will be personal friends of the dealers through friendships formed at international Forex meetings. Local financial conditions will be discussed, gossip about who is doing what in the money markets of the world will flow through the telephones.

The babel rises a few decibels as the linguists join the chorus. Rates are being quoted in French, Italian and probably German. Each operator will be dealing with the requirements of his own particular caller, whilst keeping his other ear cocked to any possible changes in rates by his colleagues as they affect their deals and look for a covering operation elsewhere.

The standard of co-operation in a team of dealers must be very high. Men of entirely different character and outlook. Yet each will dovetail into the wishes of the other. A lifted eyebrow, a nod of the head, a hand signal, a contract note pushed under a dealer's nose will all have their significance without the flow of conversation breaking.

The telex machine will have commenced its day-long chatter and the operator will be flourishing messages which require an answer. Inevitably it seems that always it is necessary to write such answers whilst carrying on an entirely separate conversation. But always the dealer must be accurate. The fatal moment when a rate is quoted without checking its accuracy will always crop up and someone somewhere in the world will benefit by a second of relaxation.

Calls from customers will be constant and will be handled with the normal courtesy, and any suggestion that perhaps the bank is a little busy will be denied with disarming cheerfulness.

With the morning well under way and his operators steadily busy the time has arrived to have a few minutes with the management.

The arrangement of the bank's finances must be discussed and the exchange dealer must be expert in every phase of the money market at home and abroad; able at a glance to supply net yields and interest arbitrage. He must know the lenders and borrowers in the international money market and have recom-

115

A telex machine and operator. The machine is called a teleprinter and resembles a typewriter. It reproduces a message and at the same time makes a similar machine elsewhere type the same message

mendations as to the credit risks involved. He may be asked to co-operate in obtaining a supply of funds in either this or another country. His opinion on probable prices will be sought and respected.

Back at his desk the flow of calls continues. Jottings of deals completed, notes to call back various customers will be strewn over his desk. By magic a cup of coffee will have appeared, to be absent-mindedly sipped as queries are dealt with, calls answered, prices listened to, accepted or refused, or counter-prices made.

The transcripts of the incoming cables of the day will be awaiting his perusal. Anything touching his department will be noted. Cables from abroad with orders for foreign exchange will be distributed to the various assistants.

There will, undoubtedly, be visitors from abroad, some very welcome, some reasonable, and some a little difficult. It is always inevitable that their arrival will coincide with a period of frantic activity. They will be received in conference rooms and their affairs gravely discussed with the background turbulence dismissed from one's mind.

It may be necessary to indulge in a long lunch with one's guests. Banking connections, reciprocal business, possibilities of mutual profit will be touched upon. By instinct the dealer would prefer, and usually has, a sandwich and back to his desk. There is no period of general lunchtime easiness in foreign exchange. Someone, somewhere will be wanting to do business, and, with the tough cut-throat international competition of today, no opportunity can be missed.

The text-books discourse widely and wisely on spot rates and forward rates. They delve deeply into the mysteries of arbitrage. No book can ever supply the answer to decision. When one can perform the classic text-book manoeuvres, life is easy. Unfortunately, especially when dealing with exchange for forward delivery, it rarely works that way. When one wants to buy dollars for, say, three months' delivery, one finds the broker offers in lieu some two months or some six months, or he cannot offer the outright date, but can offer the swap.

What shall one do! Will one of the propositions fit the book? Many questions flit through the dealer's mind. Try another broker? But the first will already have scented blood and be out scouring the market for a chance to close up a deal. To put someone else in will accentuate the effect. Take him off? He might see the opportunity to deal and go elsewhere. Try Paris? They will read a change in the market and be nipping back on another line to clobber the market under one's nose. Try Germany? Might work against marks. Can the mark dealer help? Has he something on his books which will help the arbitrage price? Questions and answers are flitting through the dealer's brain and he alone must find the answer. Meanwhile he is probably dealing with a fractious importer who is demanding last night's closing price as shown in 'The Times' for a cheque for $27·53 drawn on Milwaukee, Wis.

The afternoon pattern will continue unchanged. The arrival of the transatlantic operators at their offices will provide a fresh burst of business. Calls and cables and telex messages from across the herring pond arrive in spasms and bursts and will be dealt with by the dealers, beginning to show the strain of the day.

One is moving a ton of gold from London to Basle and turning a ten pound note for profit. No one ever sees the gold, but that is incidental. Parcels of stock certificates move across the Atlantic. A dud Italian sovereign is thrown out of a parcel displayed by a harassed cashier.

Credit departments are assured they can have funds at their disposal in some inaccessible corner of the globe. Customers are assured that the gentleman in the foreign news agency circular who has announced imminent devaluation knows ·exactly as much as anyone else.

All and sundry throughout the bank make their demands on the dealer's time and knowledge. Few go away empty-handed.

Queries large and small, petty and sometimes ridiculous, flow in all the time. Currency propositions which may or may not comply with Exchange Control must be sifted and dealt with appropriately. Never must the spoken word be other than definite, and decisions correct.

Official bank closing time has arrived and passed. Elsewhere those magic double lines are being drawn, but in the dealing room the pace remains unabated. Commodity operations are being concluded and the merchants are seeking cover for their operations from the bankers. Late resumés of the day's dealings may show the urgent need for covering operations to keep the dealer's own books in order.

Propositions and counter-propositions will still be passing to the brokers and by cable back and forth. The clock will be remorselessly ticking on and time begins to become of paramount importance.

The end of the day must eventually arrive. By 5.30 peace is beginning to prevail. The general closing-off of the day's commitments will be more or less complete. Any orders for correspondent banks in the New World will be passed along the wires. A few minutes of gossip and chat with one's colleagues before departure. The pristine morning feshness of the dealing room is by now a litter of paper jottings, pencil stubs, telex paper, brimming ashtrays and tired men.

119

9 Buying and Selling Abroad

WHEN a merchant or manufacturer sells goods abroad he hands the goods to the shipping company at his port, and when they have been loaded aboard one of the company ships he will receive a document called a Bill of Lading. The exporter or his agent makes out the bill—usually in a 'set' of two, but sometimes three—and hands it to the shipping company, whose representative signs it. In this way he acknowledges receipt of the goods detailed in the Bill of Lading. Before signing he identifies and counts the cases and crates from the exporter's marks which are stamped on them.

The Bill of Lading details the ports of departure and arrival, the name of the foreign buyer or his agent (in the case of commodities being shipped like tea or coffee, cocoa or cotton, the 'name' is simply made out 'To Order'), the special marks on the cases, the number of packages, the description of the packages (eg wooden, cardboard, fibre), the declared contents of the packages and the gross weight. The bill also embodies an undertaking by the shipping company to deliver the goods to the person named in the bill. When the bill is handed back by the shipping company the exporter sends one copy of the bill to the buyer by the first mail and the other copy or copies by later mails and/or by different routes. Sometimes one copy is sent with

120

forms of a Bill of Lading used by Atlantic Container Line. Right: the traditional ACL Bill. Left: ACL's Datafreight Receipt, which the shipper does not send to the importer. ACL transmits the details electronically across the Atlantic and they are then printed out by computer as an Arrival Notice, which is mailed to the importer before the ship arrives so that he can obtain immediate delivery of his cargo

the captain of the ship carrying the goods. In this way the importer can deal with the goods without delay.

The reason why an exporter has to prepare the Bill of Lading in a 'set' of two or three copies and dispatch each copy to the buyer by a different mail or route is a relic of the old shipping days, when the delivery of a single copy could not be guaranteed because more ships were at that time lost at sea. Nowadays, with air mail postal service, it is very unusual for the first copy not to be in the hands of the buyer before the ship arrives. However, as a precaution the second copy will give him legal title to the goods. A further margin of risk could be covered by the dispatch of a third copy. When the ship arrives at its destination and unloads its cargo the agent of the shipping company hands over the goods to the first person who presents the Bill of Lading and documents which appear to be complete and in order. This is why the exporter has to take the greatest care to see that the full set of two or three comes into the buyer's hands. If an unscrupulous person gains possession of one of the bills the genuine buyer may go to the quay for his goods only to find that they have been taken away by someone not entitled to them.

Having collected the Bill of Lading and the other shipping documents—insurance policy, invoice, etc—relating to the transaction, the exporter examines them carefully for errors and discrepancies because these could cause delay and delay costs money; then he sends them to the buyer. He now has to secure his payment. This can be done in several ways.

When he sends the documents to the importer he can also send a covering letter asking the importer to make payment by a direct remittance. If there is no arrangement between them for credit the buyer must send the money without delay. This kind of settlement is called a 'sight' payment, ie the buyer pays immediately he has sight of the documents.

The buyer's duty is now to send money to settle his account. He can send bank-notes or coin if he wishes but in practice he would not use this method because of the inconvenience and the cost of shipment and insurance. It may happen that someone in the exporter's country owes money to the buyer. If so, he can arrange for the funds to be paid over to the exporter and he will pay the balance, if any. A better way for the buyer to pay his debt is to go to his bank, who will issue their own draft, which is a banker's cheque, drawn on the bank which acts as their agent in the exporter's town or country.

There are two other ways of making payment which work something like our banker's order or a Giro transfer, but which do not pass through a clearing house. The first is a telegraphic transfer. When the parties agree to settle quickly the buyer will arrange with his bank to cable the money to the exporter or to his bank. The buyer's bank does this by sending to their agents in the seller's country a coded message by cable or wireless ordering the agents to make the payment to the exporter or direct to his bank.

If the parties do not wish to incur the expense of cabling the money the buyer's bank will send a mail transfer, generally by airmail. They write to their agents in the exporter's country instructing them to make the payment. Their letter is signed by an authorised official or officials of the bank and the agents verify the signatures by referring to specimens already in their possession.

The mail transfer payment, now most commonly used, has advantages over payment by banker's draft. Unlike the draft, it is in no danger of getting lost and perhaps falling into the wrong hands. The bank gets the exporter's receipt for the payment so he cannot claim afterwards that he has not been paid, and the buyer's bank will automatically send a confirming copy of their original instructions by a second mail to their agents, thus reducing the delay should their first letter be lost.

When a contract for the sale and purchase of goods is drawn up between an exporter and a foreign buyer the price of the goods can be quoted in one of three ways—in the buyer's own currency, in the money of the seller's country or in the currency of a third country, eg American dollars or English pounds, which may be more acceptable to the seller. When the buyer receives the shipping documents he must pay in the currency agreed. If it is his own currency his bank will issue a draft, cable transfer or mail

123

transfer in this currency. Should the contract stipulate in another
currency his bank will quote a rate of exchange and advise the
buyer how much of his own money he has to pay. He either gives
the bank his own cheque or asks the bank to charge the amount to
his banking account. At one time banks did not charge for this
service—they covered their expenses by making a small adjustment
in the rate of exchange. But since 1939 it has been a practice for
the banks to make a charge for this kind of transaction.

So far we have dealt with the way a buyer can pay immediately
he receives the shipping documents. In many contracts the
exporter allows the buyer a period of credit before he settles his
account. This period of credit does not run from the day the
exporter dispatches the shipping documents to the buyer but
from the day the importer receives them—from his first 'sight' of
them. This credit arrangement is useful to the buyer as it allows
him time to sell the goods—or part of the goods—before the
payment becomes due.

Even when the exporter and buyer arrange for settlement by
direct payment immediately the buyer receives the shipping
documents the exporter *may* still allow some credit. In this case
he is taking a risk because the buyer, in possession of the documents, has a full legal title to goods which he has not paid for.
The exporter will in fact be trusting the buyer to the value of the
goods without any form of security or legal redress. The exporter
may not wish to continue this practice and may prefer a method
by which the importer gets the documents of title to the goods
only when he has paid for them. The exporter will then use the
Bill of Exchange. This method of settlement is widely used in
many parts of the world except Scandinavia and some European
countries, who prefer to use the direct payment system.

Perhaps the best way to understand how a bill of exchange
works would be to look at it as a post-dated cheque. To satisfy a
pressing creditor someone may issue a cheque informing the
creditor that he has not sufficient funds in the banking account
to meet it at the moment. He dates the cheque some time ahead
when he will have enough money to meet it and asks the creditor
to hold it until that date before taking it into the bank. A cheque

is legally payable on demand but by post-dating it this person has made it payable on a date in the future. This is what the bill of exchange does, as this specimen shows:

'60 d/s' BILL OF EXCHANGE

London. 20th August 19. .

£2,000

Sixty days after sight of this FIRST of exchange (Second and Third of same date and tenor being unpaid) pay to my order the sum of Two thousand pounds. Shipping documents attached, to be surrendered against acceptance.

(Signed) A. N. Exporter

To C. Garcia
P.O. Box 100
Rio de Janeiro
Brazil

This is a sixty days' sight bill. Sixty days after the bill of exchange, bill of lading and other shipping documents come into the hands of the buyer he has to settle his account with the London exporter. The 'FIRST of exchange' means the bill of exchange presented to the buyer with the first batch of shipping documents. Duplicate bills of exchange accompany the other two sets of documents which, as we have seen, the exporter sends to him by later mails.

When the importer receives the bill of exchange and everything is in order he acknowledges the debt by writing his name across the face with or without the words 'Accepted' or 'Accepted at . . . Bank'. He returns the bill to the exporter and retains the shipping documents.

When the exporter receives the accepted bill from the buyer he can do one of two things. He can keep the bill until it matures and his bank will send it to the buyer or to the buyer's bank for collection, or he can discount the bill, ie sell it at something less than its face value so that he can have immediate funds for his business instead of waiting for his money until the bill falls due. The difference between the face value of the bill and the money he receives is the discount which the person or company buying the bill retains as compensation for having to wait for the money.

If the bill is drawn in the currency of the buyer's country and the exporter decides to keep it until it matures he will have at his disposal in the importer's country foreign currency which he will have to exchange into his own currency or use for buying goods in that country. The currency in that country may be unstable, which will cause the exchange rates to fluctuate. When the bill matures he may find that he has less money in terms of his own currency than he expected when he drew the bill; and unless he is sure of the buyer's integrity and financial standing he runs the risk of losing money on that score also.

But if the bill is drawn in sterling and accepted in London with the financial stability and integrity of the London acceptance houses and their stable rates of exchange, the exporter can calculate almost exactly what he will receive in sterling when the bill matures.

A London acceptance is also of great advantage if the exporter wants to discount his bill. If he took to a discount house a currency bill drawn on a foreign importer of whom they had little or no knowledge or on a little-known foreign bank, it is possible that the discount house would refuse to buy the bill. Even if they did so, the amount deducted to cover their risk would make such inroads into the exporter's profit margin that it would hardly be worth his while. On the other hand a sterling bill accepted in London could be easily discounted at a much better rate.

There is another method of settling foreign trade transactions. This is by means of bank credits. The subject of bank credits is wide and complicated and, within the scope of this book, it is only possible to touch on it very briefly.

In the transaction we are discussing let us assume that the exporter is in Britain and the buyer in, say, Brazil. When the contract for the sale and purchase of a consignment of goods has been drawn up the Brazilian importer, through his bank, will open a credit at a London bank in favour of the exporter.

Liverpool shipping terminal as the loading of cars on to the ship Atlantic Champagne gets under-way

The credit will stipulate a period of time within which the exporter has to dispatch the goods.

The exporter takes the goods to the port and hands them to the shippers in exchange for a bill of lading. Instead of sending the bill with the other shipping documents to the Brazilian buyer the exporter presents the documents at the London bank. The responsibility for seeing that the documents are in order rests with the bank. If after careful examination they find them in perfect order, they will pay the money over to the exporter.

In the same way a British bank would open a credit abroad in favour of a British importer. These banking services are not restricted to British exporters and importers. They are available to traders of good standing everywhere in the world. With the development of London-accepted bills and the growth of British bank credits for importers and exporters London has become so important as a settling place for international debts transactions that almost one-third of present-day world trade is financed by payments in sterling.

During their 'life-time', ie between the date of acceptance by a London bank and the date of maturity, people all over the world use London bills as money. They take the bills without question and in its short life one bill can be used for many transactions.

David Lloyd George, who was Chancellor of the Exchequer in 1914, wrote in his *War Memoirs:* 'The crackle of a bill on London with the signature of one of the great accepting houses was as good as the ring of gold in any port throughout the civilized world'.

10 The Coming Cashless Community

THE need for money arose with the advance of civilisation. It became easier for people to travel about and more and more goods became available. Yet it is only within the last few hundred years that money has become really important.

Although money has been used in parts of the world for nearly two thousand years, all the coins in the British Isles up to the end of the reign of Edward I, in the early fourteenth century, would not have added up to more than half a million pounds.

Money was not at that time essential as it is today and there were many self-contained communities in Britain who existed quite well without money of any kind. Thousands of peasants went through their lives possessing only a few coins at any time. They worked on the estates of the medieval landlords in return for their food, clothing and shelter. The monks in the monasteries had the same kind of existence but, while we can say that they entered into and accepted this kind of life voluntarily for religious reasons, the peasants were compelled by circumstances to live like this. When a community works for and is dependent on a master to satisfy its most primitive needs the people exist in conditions of slavery.

Perhaps the best example of this moneyless slave community is that of the Incas of Peru. When the Spaniards reached Peru

I

THE COMING CASHLESS COMMUNITY

in the sixteenth century they found an advanced people apparently living happily without money of any kind. The rulers of the community gave each man and woman a task to carry out according to his or her ability and, like the monks and peasants of Britain in the Middle Ages, they received in return food, clothing, accommodation and some simple amusements.

Apart from the rulers the people were no more than slaves. They could not change their jobs or get married without their master's permission. They were also restricted in many other ways. Without money they could not exercise any freedom of choice and their lives depended on the goodwill of their masters. Slaves in ancient Rome lived like this until the wise Romans paid their wages in money. From then on their lives changed. They were no longer slaves, they were free men, and in course of time they enjoyed the rights and privileges granted to other people.

As late as 1940 there was a completely self-contained money-less community in England. These people were the Hutterian Brotherhood, who lived in a beautiful farmhouse in Ashton Keynes, in Wiltshire. There were over a hundred members of the community, British and foreign. About half were Germans and, although they had come to Ashton Keynes with their wives and children only a short time before, they had built their own farmhouse in the traditional Cotswold style, furnishing it with articles made on their own lathes. Their staple diet was rye bread and on their farm was one of the few fields in Wiltshire where rye was grown.

The Brotherhood had a thousand fowls and over thirty head of cattle producing their own milk. They sold their surplus milk to a local factory but they made little profit. None received any wages and each family drew what they needed in the way of food and clothing from the communal store.

Late in 1940 the Brotherhood left Ashton Keynes to start a new community in Paraguay. No doubt their decision to leave Britain was prompted by the outbreak of the Second World War. With so many Germans in the community, life could have become very difficult. It is interesting to speculate, however, how they would have fared thirty years later. Would the rapid social, economic, educational and technical developments in the post-war years have compelled them to modify their way of life? Perhaps they foresaw these changes and elected to live in a less sophisticated part of the world.

In your lifetime you may see the approach of a completely moneyless society in Britain. But, unlike the Hutterians and the monks and peasants of the Middle Ages, this cashless society will come about because, by that time, money as we know it will have outlived its usefulness and will have become nothing more than a relic.

In America, housewives are already talking about the day when they will no longer need any cash to do their shopping. They foresee a time, not far distant, when they will be able to do away with their purses and buy everything they need—including the smallest items—merely by producing a credit card. In fact, in a recent experiment a man proved that he could live for three months without using any cash. With his credit card he was able to purchase everything he required—even newspapers and matches—and he did not reduce his living standards in any way.

Millions of people now use credit cards in America but it is only recently they have become so popular. Strange to say, the obstacle in the way of earlier development of the system was the housewife's reluctance to pay for her groceries with a credit card. She was happy to settle other tradesmen's accounts with a card but she preferred to pay cash for the family's food. She is gradually getting over this aversion and her change of attitude has shown the green light to the card-issuing companies who are campaigning for wider acceptance of the cards. This varies from state to state but the companies hope that soon Americans will be able to pay for everything anywhere in the country by showing their credit cards.

With this small piece of paper they can already pay their tradesmen's accounts, settle their hospital and doctor's bills and, in some of the states, even pay their taxes. In Reno they can pay their marriage fee with the card and, in Nevada, if they are unlucky enough to land in jail, they can bail their way out in the same way.

Because his parishioners carry credit cards in their pockets instead of cash the pastor of a Congregational Church in Vermont has recently placed a table in his church with a credit card machine so that his congregation can make their donations this way.

With the universal use of the credit card Americans believe that cash will eventually disappear. How far have the British gone in this direction?

In the last twenty years there has been a spectacular development in the British banking system and the rate this has grown is probably more rapid than in any other country. For many years firms have paid their salaried employees by means of monthly transfers to their banking accounts. More firms are adopting this system by transferring their lower-paid workers, who used to be paid weekly in cash, to monthly salaries. As a result Britain now issues 752 million cheques a year, covering an average total payment of nearly £13,000 a year for every man, woman and child in the country, and in every year that passes it is using 70-80 million more cheques.

Regular payments, such as rent, rates, mortgage and hire-purchase instalments, are made with banker's orders or through the Giro. The rapidly growing Inter-Bank Computer Bureau deals with over 200 million banker's orders a year and the number is increasing at the rate of 20 million every year. The National Giro, set up about two years ago, now makes transfers between accounts at the rate of nearly a million a week.

All this means that the British are using less cash and, while they may be in advance of America in extending banking services to a wider range of people, the credit card does not appear to be making as much headway.

Barclaycard, the biggest card-issuing company in Britain, now has over a million holders. If you have a Barclaycard you may run up bills to an agreed limit—usually £100. The card company settles your bills and you repay the company in full when you receive their account, or you can pay off the debt at the rate of

*The Barclaycard, produced by the largest British issuers
of credit cards*

5 per cent each month (minimum £2), and the company charges you interest on the balance outstanding.

While the Barclaycard helps you to arrange credit there are other concerns who issue cards just as a convenient means of payment and, when they send their accounts to you, you have to settle in full immediately. Diner's Club, with about 90,000 holders, and the American Express are two such companies but, at the moment, these companies do not issue cards to people with incomes lower than £2,000 a year.

The other banks do not yet issue credit cards but, to assist their customers, they have a Chequecard which guarantees payment of the customer's cheque, usually up to £30. They have issued these cards to about one in seven of their customers but the banks have to be careful about issuing them because in theory they could be committing themselves to overdrafts of up to £900 for every book of 30 cheques if the customer fails to keep sufficient funds in his account to meet the cheques he issues.

But although the number of people using credit cards has increased in recent years further expansion will depend on the integrity and the financial position of those who apply for them. If current reports are correct the position is not encouraging.

133

In a recent BBC Television broadcast of 'Tomorrow's World' it was stated that credit cards to the value of £6 million had 'bounced' in the last twelve months. This means that card-holders have run up bills to the amount agreed, which the company has paid, but the holders have failed to settle their accounts with the companies or have not kept to the monthly payment arrangement. It would appear that the growth of credit cards beyond the present 2 million or so may possibly slow down and, in the immediate future, more reliance may have to be put on the development of the banking system. But if, as predicted a short time ago by a leading trade union official, wages of unskilled workmen reach £100 a week by the turn of the century, there will be few people without a banking account and/or a credit card.

Again to reduce the need for cash, shops and stores are encouraging people to open credit accounts which are settled weekly or monthly either by cheque or by credit card. Looking further ahead you will be able to settle these accounts without a credit card or cheque. All you will do is to tell your bank which account you want to pay, quoting your own account number and the account number of the person, shop or store you are paying. The bank will pass these instructions to a central computer control and the money will automatically be transferred.

As time goes on we will see less and less money circulating, though the day when we can do away with it completely may be some distance away. But, in America, it would come as no surprise if this happened within the next decade.

11 Tales of Money ~ Strange but True

RESEARCH into the history of money often brings to light little-known stories and curiosities that cannot easily be fitted into the context of a book of this kind. Anticipating the reader's interest we are including a selection of the stories in this separate chapter. Some of them are very unusual, but they are all true.

BANK NOTE THAT SAVED A LIFE

Imprisoned for some years in an Algerian jail, without a relative or friend knowing his whereabouts, a British prisoner saved his life with a bank note. He did not bribe his guards; by dipping a sharpened splinter of wood in his own blood he wrote a message on the note and threw it out of his cell window.

After a long time the note found its way among others to a Liverpool merchant's office. Examining the notes to see if they were genuine, the cashier noticed that one bore faint traces of red handwriting. The note had long been in circulation and some of the words were indecipherable. Doggedly, however, the man stuck to his task and eventually, with the aid of a powerful magnifying glass, he made out the sentence: 'Tell John Dean of Longhill, Carlisle, that his brother is in prison in Algiers.'

The cashier immediately notified Mr Dean, who appealed for

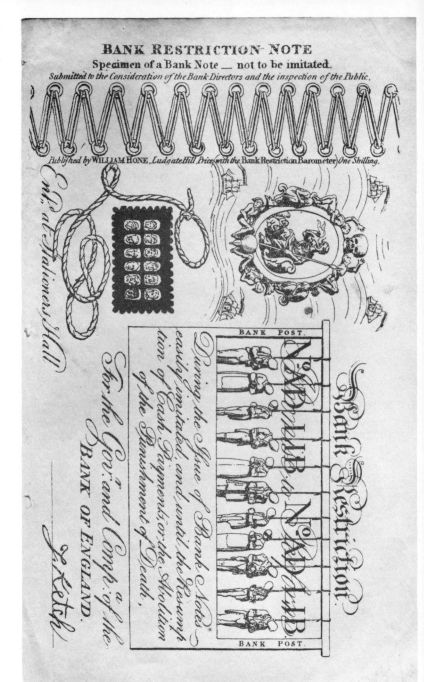

George Cruikshank drew the cartoonist drew this Bank Restriction note, signed by Jack Ketch the public executioner, at the time of Waterloo, when 307 Britons had been hanged for counterfeiting

TALES OF MONEY—STRANGE BUT TRUE

the government's help in tracing his brother. After arduous and protracted enquiries, the Foreign Office found out that the brother was a prisoner of the Dey of Algiers. Following representations the Dey released him, but he died shortly afterwards from ill-health brought on by privations and labour in the galleys.

CARICATURE BANK NOTE SAVES MANY LIVES

One day in 1818, George Cruikshank, the famous artist, was passing Newgate Prison when he noticed a large crowd gathered to witness the execution of several men and women found guilty of passing counterfeit one-pound notes—a crime then punishable by death.

Moved by pity and shame, Cruikshank produced a note in the form of a cartoon portraying a row of criminals hanging by the neck from the gallows and a figure of Britannia surrounded by the transport ships that carried to Australia those criminals who managed to escape the death penalty.

His publisher printed and exhibited the caricature notes in his window. So great was the demand for them that soldiers dispersed the crowds round the shop. Alarmed by this publicity for the severity of the punishment meted out for this crime, the directors of the Bank of England hurriedly discontinued the issue of one-pound notes. In this way counterfeiting of the note was brought to an end and many unfortunates were saved from the Newgate gallows.

SAGA OF THE RUSSIAN GOLD HOARD

In Russia in 1917, during the First World War, the air was full of rumours—'whispers like the chattering of birds', to quote a writer of the time—whispers about immense hoards of gold flitting about from place to place all over the vast country. The people did not know whether the whispers they heard were a reality or a myth and a year went by before the truth came out.

When the Germans threatened Petrograd, where the State treasure was stored, the Russians moved it to Kazan where, during the revolution, it fell into the hands of the Bolsheviks.

K

An anti-Bolshevik group called the People's Army captured Kazan and took the treasure to Samara. When the Bolsheviks drove them eastwards they moved the gold again to Omsk, where they placed it in the vaults of the State Bank. This was just another resting place. Only when the fight for Russia ended did the treasure reach its final destination. At this point the gold was examined by representatives of the military forces (including a British contingent) who were helping the White Russians in their struggle against the Bolsheviks. They went to the State Bank where they saw tier upon tier of shelves stacked with wooden boxes. Some boxes were full of dull gold nuggets all about the same size. In other boxes were gold coins of every nationality, such as English sovereigns, Spanish twenty-peseta pieces, French twenty-franc pieces. One box contained a ball of gold one foot in diameter. The treasure weighed about 500 tons.

Admiral Kolchak, the leader of the White forces, decided to send the treasure from Omsk to the coast. The train in which the gold was to travel was ready with soldiers of the Hampshire Regiment in control charge but, for some reason, Kolchak would not release the gold. Two months later the Bolsheviks threatened Omsk and the treasure was on the move again. Whispers again spread like flames through Siberia. The treasure travelled hundreds of miles further east and eventually reached Irkutsk. The journey took several weeks and on the way some of the coaches disappeared. Kolchak had helped himself to the gold so that he could continue his resistance to the Bolsheviks.

Shortly afterwards Kolchak's resistance collapsed and he had to hand the gold to the revolutionaries. It then started on its last journey westwards over thousands of miles to Moscow. When it arrived after a year's wandering and reduced by depredations on its long journey it was still worth over seventy million pounds.

MAN WHO PAID THE NATIONAL DEBT

James Swan was born in 1754 in Fifeshire, Scotland, and emigrated as a youth to America. He settled in Boston and became a wealthy merchant by the time he was thirty. In 1787 he went to live in France where he continued in business as a merchant accumulating more wealth and gaining influence.

At that time the United States owed France about two million dollars, money which she had borrowed to help her over her difficulties during the revolution of the colonists. This amount is trifling compared with national debts today but two hundred years ago it was a substantial sum of money. Swan decided to pay this debt out of his own pocket and, in 1795, he reported to the United States government that the entire American debt was paid and did not exist any more.

Thirteen years afterwards the French put him into a debtor's prison because he did not meet a court judgment against him for $150,000 which a German firm alleged he owed them. Swan denied that he owed the money and rather than pay he accepted what was virtually a life sentence.

He served 22 years in the Sainte Pelagie prison and the French released him at the outbreak of the Revolution in 1830. Three days after his release he died.

HOW THE BANK OF ENGLAND PAID A £30,000 NOTE TWICE

One of the Bank's directors who wanted to purchase an estate drew from the Bank a single note for £30,000. When he arrived home that day he placed the note on the mantelpiece and, as he was doing so, he was called from the room. When he came back a few moments later the note had disappeared. Nobody could have taken it because no-one had entered the room while he was out and he was sure that the note had fallen into the fire.

The Bank believed his story and gave him a second note on the understanding that the first, if ever found, should be returned to them. Thirty years afterwards, when the director had been dead a long time, a stranger came to the Bank and presented the missing note.

As it was payable to bearer, the Bank was compelled to meet the obligation, and thereby lost £30,000. They found out afterwards that a builder had bought the director's house, which he demolished. During demolition he found the note hidden in a crevice in the chimney.

MYSTERY OF THE WANDERING MILLION

Many of you know or have heard about the famous 'Lutine' Bell at Lloyd's Register of Shipping, in London. The bell used to be rung when there was a disaster at sea, but now it is sounded mainly when an important announcement, usually of a ceremonial nature, is to be made. Not so generally well known as the bell is the mysterious story of the wreck of the naval frigate *La Lutine* from which it was recovered.

On 19 October 1799 a London paper gave the grave news that *La Lutine* under the command of a Captain Skynner had been lost in a gale on the outward bank of the Fly Island Passage in Holland a few days earlier. The paper further reported that *La Lutine* had sailed from Yarmouth on the morning of 9 October with several passengers aboard and an immense quantity of treasure bound for Texel, in Holland. A strong tide had made it impossible for Captain Skynner to avoid the danger and in such a night he could not be given any assistance. At dawn next morning a search was made for the frigate but no trace could be found. She had broken into pieces and everybody on board had perished except two survivors who died from exhaustion shortly afterwards.

This was the gist of the newspaper report, but the disappearance of *La Lutine* has since been shrouded in mystery, leaving many questions still unanswered.

Most accounts of the occurrence agree that the frigate was bound for Texel with bullion to pay the British troops who were then in Holland but Admiralty records do not confirm this. In fact the records make it clear that the Admiralty had not ordered her to sail to Texel but to Hamburg. They also show that the treasure on board did not belong to the British Government but to a group of London merchants.

How was it then that *La Lutine*, under orders to sail to Hamburg with an experienced commander, foundered off the coast of Holland? Why did her skipper, having run into bad

*Lutine Bell at Lloyd's Register of Shipping, London,
saved from the mysterious wreck of the naval frigate* La
Lutine

weather, not give a wide berth to this dangerous coast, which was a graveyard strewn with wrecks? Another mystery: Why was a powerful British naval frigate used to carry bullion and cash for private persons?

It soon came to light that the officer responsible for changing *La Lutine's* orders was Admiral Lord Duncan, then commanding the flagship *Kent* in Yarmouth Roads. In his letter of 9 October to the Admiralty he said that merchants wishing to send bullion to the continent had asked him for a naval ship to carry this large sum of money. As there was no packet ship available, he had agreed to their request and had ordered Captain Skynner to take *La Lutine* to Cuxhaven with the bullion and with mail for the continent that was awaiting transport, and then to go on to Stromness. Before his letter reached the Admiralty the frigate and its treasures lay broken on the sandbanks of Holland. This poses the further question: What was the real reason why Admiral Lord Duncan should have accepted the responsibility of countermanding Admiralty orders and re-directing the ship to Cuxhaven, and why was he not censured for the disaster resulting from a decision he made personally without seeking Admiralty approval?

All the Admiralty did was to state their 'great concern at the very unfortunate accident' and to issue instructions that everything possible should be done to recover 'the stores' from the ill-fated frigate. This was the end of the incident as far as they were concerned.

Most of the treasure on board was insured with the underwriters at Lloyd's, who made the payment to the owners without delay. This shows the stability and resources of Lloyd's, even at the end of the eighteenth century.

By paying the claim Lloyd's were entitled to the treasure if it could be salvaged. But this did not seem a hopeful proposition. At the time Britain was at war with the Netherlands and, even afterwards, the prospects were poor because this area is continually exposed to bad weather, making dredging operations possible only for a short time every year.

In 1857 a Dutch company made a serious effort to salvage

the treasure by using steam suction dredgers. They agreed to pay over one-half of everything they found to Lloyd's. They dredged for two years before finding the bell and rudder, which they sent to Lloyd's, and bullion amounting to about £22,000.

Shortly afterwards a great gale closed the channel and buried all hopes of tracing the wreck. So a million pounds of treasure lie for ever in the sands of the Zuyder Zee.

WORLD'S MOST CURIOUS CHEQUE

When you issue a cheque you instruct your bank to pay a certain sum of money to the person named in the cheque whenever he demands it within a reasonable period of time, usually within six months. There is no stipulation as to what you use to write the cheque or what you write it on. A bank cheque form is not legally necessary and, if you ever find that you have forgotten your cheque book and want to pay somebody, you can make the cheque out on a piece of paper, sign it, and the bank will honour your piece of paper.

To emphasise this point teachers of banking used to tell their pupils that you could make out a cheque in red paint on a white cow and, if you brought the cow to the bank, they could not legally refuse payment of the written order.

A customer of the Californian banking firm of Palmer, Cook & Co called at the bank to withdraw $28,000 from his account to make an urgent payment. At that time, over a hundred years ago, it was the custom for an official of the bank to sign cheques for large amounts. Mr Joseph C. Palmer, a partner in the bank, had this job but he was away at a timber yard some three or four miles distant.

The customer raced to Mr Palmer and told him what he wanted. Mr Palmer could find neither pen, pencil, ink nor paper, and there was no time to send back to the bank for a cheque. He did not hesitate. Looking round the yard for a flat piece of timber, he wrote out the cheque on it for $28,000 with a piece of red chalk. The customer took the 'cheque' to the bank, where it was cashed without question.

HER MONEY WAS ALL RIGHT

Some years before the outbreak of the First World War an elderly lady deposited three hundred golden sovereigns in a small country bank. When war started she was concerned about her money and went to the bank to draw it out. The cashier handed her £300 and interest in the newly issued £1 treasury notes with some silver and copper. She refused the notes saying that she had given the bank golden sovereigns and she wanted sovereigns in return.

At that time the bank was legally bound to pay her in sovereigns if she asked for them. Her request placed it in a dilemma. It had only a few of the coins on hand at that time and the only solution was to try to obtain more of the coins to meet the old lady's request. She was asked to call again in a few days' time and was assured that the sovereigns would be there when she came back. The manager delegated a clerk to try to find the sovereigns. The clerk hired a horse and trap and scoured the countryside, asking all the banks within thirty miles if they could spare some sovereigns. With ten pounds from one bank and twenty pounds from another and so on he just managed to rake in the three hundred with a few minutes to spare.

The old lady called at the bank as arranged and the cashier told her that they had the sovereigns. She pulled out her white apron and asked him to pour the sovereigns into it. She took one long look at the coins and then said 'I see that my money is all right. You can have it back again now.'

'FROM TINY STREAMS . . .'

When the private bank Child & Co opened its new building in Fleet Street in 1880 a small newsboy came in, clutching a few pennies in his hand, and asked to see the manager.

'What is that for?' asked the manager, eyeing the handful of pence.

The boy pointed to the notice on the door, 'Child's Bank'.

This story has a moral for bankers. Such small sums of money, trifling in themselves, all together form a substantial part of the vast sum of money in our banks today.

THE BELLS OF CALCUTTA

If you go to Calcutta and stay at a hotel overlooking a busy street you will perhaps not be able to sleep very easily. Long after the traffic has died down you will hear a continuous clanging, like the jingling of small bells. You go to the window and look at the street, and you see groups of Indian street traders gesticulating and arguing fiercely with their late-night customers. They are discussing in a noisy way whether they should take the rupees offered to them for their goods. Counterfeiting is so rife in Calcutta that every coin is suspect. A rough and ready way to find out if a coin is genuine or not is to bang it hard on the pavement and listen to the clang. A genuine rupee has a different ring from the counterfeit article but forging is so clever that it is often difficult to detect one ring from another. This is what all the argument is about.

ACKNOWLEDGEMENTS

The author wishes to thank Professor E. Victor Morgan of the University of Manchester for his kind permission to use material from his book *A History of Money;* and the Institute of Bankers for allowing the quotation of part of the chapter 'A Foreign Exchange Dealer' from their booklet *A Day in the Life of a Banker;* and the Bank Education Service, the Institute of Bankers, and Atlantic Container Line Service Ltd for advice about the text.

INDEX